Inspired Finance

Inspired Finance

The Role of Faith in Microfinance and International Economic Development

Michael Looft
Kiva Microfunds, USA

First published 2014 by
PALGRAVE MACMILLAN

Palgrave Macmillan in the UK is an imprint of Macmillan Publishers Limited, registered in England, company number 785998, of Houndmills, Basingstoke, Hampshire RG21 6XS.

Palgrave Macmillan in the US is a division of St Martin's Press LLC, 175 Fifth Avenue, New York, NY 10010.

Palgrave Macmillan is the global academic imprint of the above companies and has companies and representatives throughout the world.

Palgrave® and Macmillan® are registered trademarks in the United States, the United Kingdom, Europe and other countries.

ISBN 978–1–137–45077–7

A catalogue record for this book is available from the British Library.

Library of Congress Cataloging-in-Publication Data
Looft, Michael, 1971–
Inspired finance : the role of faith in microfinance and international economic development / Michael Looft.
pages cm
Summary:"Inspired Finance argues that much of the world's poor need access to financial services through vehicles such as microfinance rather than a continued reliance on charity. It demonstrates how modern microfinance traces its roots to various religious traditions, exploring the tension between charity and self-reliance in those traditions. Through thoughtful investigation and engaging case studies, Inspired Finance examines the impact these historical religious legacies have had on designing and developing financial services for the poor. Ultimately, Inspired Finance challenges you to consider how these religious influences can be restructured to help a rapidly growing industry target the poor in a way that truly helps them rise out of poverty, while at the same time respecting their inherent worth and dignity"— Provided by publisher.
ISBN 978–1–137–45077–7 (hardback)
1. Finance—Religious aspects. 2. Microfinance. 3. Charities.
4. Poverty—Religious aspects. 5. Economic development—Religious aspects. I. Title.
HG103.L66 2014
332—dc23   2014025009

Typeset by MPS Limited, Chennai, India.

Transferred to Digital Printing in 2014

For my beautiful son Zachary, who inspires me every day

Contents

List of Figures

Acknowledgments

I am very grateful to Dr M. Christian Green for introducing me to the primary source literature at Harvard Divinity School and for her extremely constructive comments and guidance on the initial draft of this book. Thank you also to Rev. Dr Emily Click, Rev. Dudley Rose, and Dr Milton Kornfeld at Harvard Divinity School for their enduring guidance and advisement throughout my time there. I am grateful to Kim Wilson and Dr Ibrahim Warde at the Fletcher School of Law and Diplomacy for teaching me many of the microfinance and Islamic banking concepts that I brought to my work and explored in this book. A very special thanks goes to Rev. Dr Frederic J Muir, William Easterly, Dr Muhammad Yunus, Brett Matthews, and Stuart Rutherford for teaching me to think differently about microfinance and international development.

A special thanks to Juan Mejia for introducing me to my first work experiences in microfinance in the Guatemalan highlands. Thank you to the members of the Unitarian Universalist Association that gave me the opportunity to participate in foundational economic development experiences in India, Romania, and the Philippines: Rev. Eric Cherry, Cathy Cordes, Eileen Higgins, Dr Richard Ford, Bob Guerrero, Rev. Rebecca Siennes, Rev. Nihal Attanayake, and Rev. Helpme Mohrmen. Thank you to Dr Jon Bart from Village Hope International for the opportunity to learn what works and what does not work in rural Sierra Leone.

Thank you to Cristina Trullols from the IE Business School; Aimee Dibbens, my editor at Palgrave Macmillan; Gemma d'Arcy Hughes from Palgrave Macmillan; and to the following people and institutions that contributed in one way or another to the formation and substance of this book: Teresa Yung, Michael Mazur, Asasah, Tabinda Jaffery, Agro Capital Management, Stephen Wright, Oleg Osauluk, Yayasan Sosial Bina Sejahtera, Father Charlie Burrows, Cristina Widiantarti, Center for Community Transformation, Ruth Callanta, Leah Katigbak, Michelle Taway, Arthur Trinidad, Chris Dunford, Freedom from Hunger, Pew Forum, Kara Levy, and Adrienne Kelly. And finally, a very special thank you to my colleagues and friends at Kiva Microfunds, who have taught me much about microfinance and passion in the unique way that only Kiva can do.

Introduction

"Can anybody remember when the times were not
hard, and money not scarce?"[1]

Ralph Waldo Emerson

Many of the world's poor have virtually no way to access the financial services they need to overcome poverty. The term "money lending" typically does not evoke images of spirituality and community
building, but that is exactly what has been happening as a result of
people extending small loans to the poor. Over the past forty years,
microfinance institutions have been at the forefront of helping to
reduce poverty by giving the poor a chance to access microcredit
loans as well as other financial services, such as savings and insurance that traditional banks will not extend to them.[2] The power of
microfinance lies in the collaborative relationships that it fosters
with the poor in contrast to the paternalism inherent in traditional

---

[1] RWE.org, The Works of Ralph Waldo Emerson, "Chapter VII Works and
Days," http://rwe.org/complete-works/vii—society-and-solitude/chapter-vii–
works-and-days (accessed 2 January 2014).
[2] The term *microfinance* refers to the provision of financial services to the
poor and low-income sectors of the economy. These include credit, savings,
insurance, retirement accounts, access to fund transfers, and other financial
services that consumers in developed countries readily enjoy. It may also
include financial literacy, training, and other social services that help clients
increase their livelihoods. The term *microcredit* refers to the distribution of
loans to the poor and can be considered a subset of microfinance.

1

charity. These microfinance-based relationships offer people a chance to rise out of their impoverished conditions by giving them the tools and support they need to chart a new course in life and to achieve financial stability.

Faith communities and organizations have played an extensive and important role in supporting microfinance from its beginnings and sustaining other international economic development efforts for the past several hundred years. For many people, this represents a profound expression of love for one's neighbor. Engaging in microfinance has helped faith communities to practice generosity and to recognize the inherent worth and dignity of every human being. In exploring the intersection between faith and international economic development, this book will assert and support the following arguments:

1. Most of the world's poor need access to financial services rather than a continued reliance on charity.
2. Faith communities have a long history of inspiring and promoting models used in international economic development that have heavily influenced modern microfinance.
3. Enduring issues rooted in faith need to be re-evaluated in order for international economic development to be made beneficial and effective over the long term.
4. Faith can play an active and inspirational role in promoting healthy international economic development and perhaps helping to reshape the global financial industry as a whole.

In order to explore these arguments, Chapter 1 will review biblical and secular scholarship around charity to define its limits and to make the case for financial services for the poor (microfinance) as a healthy expression of giving to the poor. Chapter 2 will then introduce the reader to the history of financial services for the poor, demonstrating how its many strands originated from faith communities and have slowly evolved into modern microfinance. Chapters 3 through 5 will focus on persistent economic issues rooted in faith that continue to present challenges to modern microfinance and international economic development in general. Chapter 6 will take a deeper look at a spectrum of organizations engaging in microfinance that have drawn their inspiration from a particular faith, illustrating the power this connection has had on reaching the poor. The final chapter will quickly summarize major concepts explored in the book, with ideas for how readers can become directly involved in supporting financial services for the poor.

Before diving into this book, it is important to clarify how the term "poor" will be used in this context. In 1995, the Consultative Group to Assist the Poorest and the Microcredit Summit Campaign Committee formally defined a "poor" person as someone who lives below the poverty line and the "poorest" as someone in the bottom half of those below the poverty line. While this poverty line varies by country, more than half of the world's population indeed lives on less than $2 a day—which is shown in Figure I.1 and often cited to capture the strata defining the poorest of the poor. The poverty pyramid shown in Figure I.1 further delineates the various economic activities undertaken by the poor, and serves as a useful model for determining the appropriateness of certain financial products.[3]

Figure I.1 Poverty pyramid in microfinance
Source: © 2012 Center for Community Transformation

[3] Systems and Us, "How Kiva Serves the Poorest," Courtesy of Center for Community Transformation, 26 July 2012, http://systemsandus.com/2012/07/26/how-kiva-serves-the-poorest/ (accessed 5 January 2014).

One important point to keep in mind while reading this book is that international economic development methods such as microfinance are not specifically designed to address *all* of the fundamental needs of the poor and the poorest of the poor. For many people throughout the world the basics of survival such as food, shelter, clothing, and proper medical care must first be met before establishing a solid connection to financial services. Introducing models to help people to generate and to preserve wealth over the long term is possible *only after* those basic needs are met. So, in examining the poverty pyramid figure it is important to keep in mind that, depending on the country and market context and the situation of the people living in it, microfinance may not *yet* be in a position to serve them. However, the ultimate goal of microfinance is to ensure that *everyone* acquires fair access to the same types of financial services that those in the developed world already enjoy.

1
Charity Revisited

"Charity is injurious unless it helps the recipient to become independent of it."[1]

John D. Rockefeller

In his book *God's Politics*, the evangelical leader Jim Wallis reminds his readers that one-sixteenth of the verses in the New Testament relate to the poor or the subject of money.[2] To drive home his point that society as a whole needs to address poverty alleviation, he adds his own twist on a popular anonymous quote, "a society's integrity is judged, not by its wealth and power, but by how it treats its most vulnerable members."[3] While biblical authority might hold sway over adherents who find inspiration in the words of the prophets, people who do not ground their values in a Judeo-Christian or another faith-based context may instead find guidance in Aristotle's appeals to universal ideas. To present a model of generosity that gives the recipients of that generosity the power to shape their own lives, this chapter will trace both biblical and secular scholarship around charitable giving. This ethical model contains two primary foundations. First, although there will always be poor people in the world,

---

[1] Forbes.com, "Thoughts on the Business of Life", John D Rockefeller, http://thoughts.forbes.com/thoughts/charity-john-d-rockefeller-jr-charity-is-injurious (accessed 31 December 2013).
[2] Jim Wallis, *God's Politics: Why the Right Gets It Wrong and the Left Doesn't Get It* (New York: HarperSanFrancisco, 2005), 212.
[3] Wallis, *God's Politics*, 236.

they need and deserve generosity. Second, that generosity must manifest in ways that help the poor to become self-sufficient and to flourish through their own efforts. This chapter will cover these two elements, and will end by introducing microfinance as a giving method that is not only aligned with this ethical model, but also a very effective way to help the poor lift themselves out of poverty.

Loving one's neighbor

When the Pharisees asked Christ which commandment was most important, he answered, "[L]ove the Lord your God with all your heart, and with all your soul, and with all your mind, and with all your strength. The second is this: 'You shall love your neighbor as yourself.' There is no commandment greater than these.[4] The words he uses, "love your neighbor as yourself," are first found in God's interaction with Moses in Leviticus.[5] Some scholars argue that the gospel writers perceived Christ to be the new Moses, sent to remind people that this old law is rooted in love.[6] Closer inspection of the passages in the Gospel of Mark, also repeated in Matthew[7] and in Luke[8], reveals that when asked for one commandment, Christ provided two, nevertheless framing them in unified terms. If loving one's neighbor depends on an initial love for God, it also relies on an unconditional self-love[9] that must come first.

If one believes that God is both outside and within an individual, the progression from God to self to others illuminates an iterative process. In other words, God's love passes through a person, onto other people, then back through God to complete the circuit. By claiming "all the Law and the Prophets hang on these two commandments,"[10]

---

[4] Mark 12:30–31 (Revised Standard Version).
[5] Leviticus 19:18 (Revised Standard Version).
[6] The Ancient Greek word used for love in both Mark 12:30–31 and Leviticus 19:18 (Septuagint Greek text) is *agape* ($\alpha\gamma\acute{\alpha}\pi\eta$), which means love in a divine, unconditional sense—as opposed to *eros* (romantic love), or *philia* (friendship).
[7] Matthew 22:37–39 (Revised Standard Version).
[8] Luke 10:27 (Revised Standard Version).
[9] Love of oneself here most likely resembles an inward affinity with one's soul, rather than the pejorative meaning of selfishness.
[10] Matthew 22:40 (Revised Standard Version).

Christ ensured that everything else in his teaching would conform to these two commandments. To follow Christ meant that personal actions had to conform to this standard.

Loving and showing respect for one's neighbor also traces its roots to the Hellenistic notion of the stranger. The Ancient Greek word for stranger also meant "guest" and "host," implying a unique relationship that binds people together rather than marking a separation.[11] Arguably, the ethical norm of this stranger-host relationship is a central theme in Homer's two epics the *Iliad* and the *Odyssey*. As Homer wrote, "All strangers and wanderers are sacred in the sight of Zeus (Book 6, Line 207)."[12]

In the *Iliad*, Paris's abduction of Helen, the Spartan King Menelaus's wife, violates the hospitality covenant between guest and host, prompting the Greeks to besiege Troy. The *Odyssey* not only narrates Odysseus's long venture home after the war, but also the numerous occasions when he and other characters appear as guests in the homes of people they have just met. Despite Odysseus's disguised appearance as a beggar when he finally returns home to Ithaca, the swineherd, Eumaeus, treats him with the same respect he would afford to any person. Similarly, when Odysseus's son Telemachus arrives in Sparta, King Menelaus entertains him even though there is a wedding taking place. Homer's epics demonstrate the harmonious host-stranger relationship with examples of treating the tacit covenant with respect. However, the Greek response to Helen's abduction and Odysseus's slaughter of the suitors—fueled by his disappointment at their callous behavior while he was away at war—serve as insightful examples of how badly things can go when people compromise the stranger-host relationship.

Christ takes the concept of the host-stranger relationship a step further in the parable of the Good Samaritan, found in the Gospel of Luke, where he illustrates the proper treatment of even those to whom one has no formal connection. In the gospel, it is not Christ, but an expert in the law who delivers the commandments of loving

---

[11] The Ancient Greek word ξένος (xenos) provides the root prefix for some English words related to strangers (e.g. "xenophobia").

[12] Homer and Richmond Alexander Lattimore, *the Odyssey of Homer* (New York: Harper Perennial, 1991), 107.

God and loving one's neighbor as oneself. However, when he asks Christ, "Who is my neighbor?" he receives this response:

> A man was going down from Jerusalem to Jericho, and he fell among robbers, who stripped him and beat him, and departed, leaving him half dead. Now by chance a priest was going down that road; and when he saw him he passed by on the other side. So likewise a Levite, when he came to the place and saw him, passed by on the other side. But a Samaritan, as he journeyed, came to where he was; and when he saw him, he had compassion, and went to him and bound up his wounds, pouring on oil and wine; then he set him on his own beast and brought him to an inn, and took care of him. And the next day he took out two denarii[d] and gave them to the innkeeper, saying, "Take care of him; and whatever more you spend, I will repay you when I come back." "Which of these three, do you think, proved neighbor to the man who fell among the robbers?" He said, "The one who showed mercy on him." And Jesus said to him, "Go and do likewise."[13]

Both the priest and the Levite were thought to have divine authority: the priest as a presumed representative of God on earth, and the Levite because his tribe was charged with ministering to the priests.[14] If anyone should have stopped to help the dying man, it ought to have been one of those two. Yet it is the Samaritan, a supposed enemy of the Israelites,[15] who showed his love for the stranger. He not only provided food and shelter to the man who would have surely died, but also gave the innkeeper extra money to continue supporting him. As Christ's parable emphasizes, the commandment to love one's neighbor was a call for the disciples to notice the people in their lives most in need of help, especially the ones they would prefer to avoid.

Arguably, Christ's central message to his followers was that they should help those who are worse off than they are. For Christians, when the Son of Man returns, the inheritors of the kingdom of God will be the ones who fed the hungry, clothed the poor, and took in

---

[13] Luke 10:29–37 (Revised Standard Version).
[14] Numbers 18:6 (Revised Standard Version).
[15] Luke 9:52 (Revised Standard Version).

the stranger.[16] The Sermon on the Mount served as a blessing both to meek strangers and to their merciful hosts. Here he admonished those who give to the needy to do so in secret, without sounding off trumpets of self-righteousness.[17] For Christ, we should love our neighbor, whether he is poor, downtrodden, or neglected on the side of the road.

Jim Wallis addresses a common misinterpretation of Christ's statement, "The poor you will always have with you, and you can help them any time you want. But you will not always have me."[18] Many people rely on the first clause of this passage to assuage any guilt for either ignoring the poor or even placing the blame on them for their own poverty.[19] Wallis underscores the context of the passage, wherein Christ is protecting a woman who pours expensive ointment on him while he is seated at a table in a leper's home. The disciples criticize her for wasting money on the ointment, rather than spending it on the poor. Christ is reminding them that the mission of helping the poor is ongoing, and that people can still be generous with the poor yet extravagant in their worship of God. Furthermore, as Wallis has pointed out, Christ grounded his teaching in Deuteronomy:[20]

> If there is among you a poor man, one of your brethren, in any of your towns within your land which the Lord your God gives you, you shall not harden your heart or shut your hand against your poor brother, but you shall open your hand to him, and lend him sufficient for his need, whatever it may be. Take heed lest there be a base thought in your heart, and you say, "The seventh year, the year of release is near," and your eye be hostile to your poor brother, and you give him nothing, and he cry to the Lord against you, and it be sin in you. You shall give to him freely, and your heart shall not be grudging when you give to him; because for this the Lord your God will bless you in all your work and in all that you undertake. For the poor will never cease out of the land; therefore I command you, You shall open wide your hand to your brother, to the needy and to the poor, in the land.[21]

---

[16] Matthew 25:34–40 (Revised Standard Version).
[17] Matthew 6:1–3 (Revised Standard Version).
[18] Mark 14:7 (Revised Standard Version).
[19] Wallis, *God's Politics*, 211.
[20] Wallis, *God's Politics*, 210–211.
[21] Deuteronomy 15:7–11 (Revised Standard Version).

The poor might always be in the land, but the God of the Bible commanded people to give generously to the poor rather than passing by and leaving them for dead.

Aristotle and generosity

Aristotle's systematic ethical system has served as a foundation for theological and secular thinkers for over two millennia. In fact, his thought has been so influential that the well-known British analytic philosopher Elizabeth Anscombe's 1958 paper entitled "Modern Moral Philosophy" argued for a return to Aristotle's conception of virtue ethics as a guide for morality.[22] This view indicates that his ancient ethical system might still serve as an excellent guide to resolving modern dilemmas—regardless of the time period.

In the *Nicomachean Ethics*, Aristotle asserted that the aim of a self-controlled person is to do what is noble and in accordance with reason (1119b15),[23] thereby achieving *eudaimonia*.[24] The word "eudaimonia," etymologically a conjunction of the Ancient Greek words for "well" and "spirit," has often been translated as "happy"—but the true meaning in its fullest sense may better be captured in the idea of "human flourishing."[25] Aristotle characterizes eudaimonia as not simply one good thing among many others, but rather the most desirable of all things—the highest human good and arguably the ultimate purpose of ethics and political philosophy. This comes about through living a complete life where habitual actions are in accordance with excellence in virtue (1098a16).[26] Eudaimonia is not

---

[22] Elizabeth Anscombe, "Modern Moral Philosophy," in *Philosophy*, vol. 33, no. 124 (January 1958).

[23] Aristotle and Martin Ostwald, *Nicomachean Ethics* (Englewood Cliffs, NJ: Prentice Hall, 1992), 82.

[24] Ancient Greek: εὐδαιμονία.

[25] Liddell and Scott offer the following alternative translations for εὐδαιμονία (eudaimonia) from the Greek Ionic dialect: *prosperity, good fortune, wealth, weal, happiness*. This suggests that fully flourishing as a human being and being happy are somewhat tied to achieving material wealth or fortune (though not ultimately dependent on it). See Henry Liddell and Robert Scott, *An Intermediate Greek-English Lexicon* (New York: Oxford University Press, 2001), 323.

[26] Aristotle, *Nicomachean Ethics*, 19.

some passing emotion, such as a single sunny day, but a state of mind achieved by maintaining an uncorrupted soul through repeating virtuous actions over the course of a lifetime. While virtuous actions do not necessarily ensure eudaimonia, for Aristotle it is not possible to achieve this condition *without* virtuous actions. One cannot find bliss without being good. Incidentally, this bliss means participating in the activities and fortunes of the gods; and that activity is best spent in quiet contemplation as to ensure continued happiness (1178b21).[27]

To ensure a healthy relationship between benefactor and recipient, Aristotle noted that the noble person will give in a correct manner that is "to the right people, the right amount, at the right time, and do everything else that is implied in correct giving (1120a23)."[28] In his ethical system, virtue lay at the mean between excess and deficiency—sometimes referred to as the "Golden Mean." Hence, generosity represents the virtuous position between extravagance (an excess of giving) and stinginess (both a deficiency of giving and perhaps an excess of taking) (1121a13).[29] Furthermore, the virtuous person derives pleasure in doing the right thing, making eudaimonia possible for both himself and even others. Finally, Aristotle concluded that even the extravagant person is far superior to the stingy one because he is helpful to many, while the stingy man helps nobody, not even himself (1120a28).[30]

Cicero later expanded Aristotle's application of generosity to virtue ethics by considering implications for the different ways people give to the poor. He defined helping others as either through personal effort or by giving money. Giving money is the easier of the two, especially for a rich person. Since personal effort requires more than merely a draft on one's financial capital, he deemed it nobler. Cicero relegated the authority for deciding on gifts and other monetary expenditures to the Aristotelian Golden Mean.[31] In keeping this view, he said that the greatest privilege of wealth is the opportunity it affords for doing good, without sacrificing one's fortune.[32] In rendering helpful service

---

[27] Aristotle, *Nicomachean Ethics*, 293.
[28] Aristotle, *Nicomachean Ethics*, 84.
[29] Aristotle, *Nicomachean Ethics*, 87.
[30] Aristotle, *Nicomachean Ethics*, 87.
[31] Marcus Tullius Cicero and Michael Grant, "On Duties II," *in On the Good Life* (Penguin Classics. Harmondsworth: Penguin, 1971), 154.
[32] Cicero, *On the Good Life*, 156.

to people, he admonished others to look at their neighbors' circum-stances and not simply at their characters. Although those without possessions may not be able to repay the favor in practical terms, they can at least repay with their hearts.[33]

Though he allowed that people should sometimes make gifts of money, Cicero warned of setting limits on the amount. First, he argued, money may corrupt people if they view the gift as a form of bribe. Second, lavish giving sometimes dissipates entire inheritances, therefore perhaps even obliging the giver to steal from others. Third, this type of giving accustoms people to being subsidized, so they are bound to want more, while also attracting those who have not yet received this money. He repeated the common phrase of the time, "bounty is a bottomless pit," to add weight to his argument that excessive giving can lead to enablement.[34] By explicating Aristotle's definition of generosity, Cicero outlined healthy boundaries for giving by calling attention to the problems associated with reckless benevo-lence. A generous person can do much to help others, but must main-tain a certain degree of restraint and must also recognize the possible implications of his or her giving.

Here we uncover the main difference between the applications of Christian and Aristotelian ethics to the concept of generosity. The Aristotelian view calls for pragmatism and restraint, while Christ asked his followers to go deeper and rethink their own relationship and attachments to wealth. When a rich, young ruler asked how he could inherit eternal life, Christ began listing some of the com-mandments. Unsatisfied with this flat response, the ruler explained that keeping those commandments had not done much to help him. Christ replied, "You still lack one thing. Sell everything you have and give to the poor, and you will have treasure in heaven. Then come, follow me." According to the gospels, when the man heard this, "he became very sad, because he was a man of great wealth."[35] To inherit eternal life, and presumably to be happy, the ruler must sell off his worldly goods and give the proceeds to the poor. As biblical scholar

---

[33] Cicero, *On the Good Life*, 158.
[34] Cicero, *On the Good Life*, 148–149.
[35] Luke 18:20–23 (Also: Matthew 19:20–22 and Mark 10:21–22) (Revised Standard Version).

Ulrich Luz has pointed out, "the call to renounce possessions and give to the poor must be understood as the concrete enactment of the command to love one's neighbor."[36]

Christ was not advocating that everyone give up all of his or her possessions; in fact, he commended the tax collector Zacchaeus for announcing his intention to give only half of his possessions to the poor.[37] What made the ruler different from the tax collector was his *attachment* to possessions. To love his neighbor meant ultimately giving up what stood between him and God, and until he gave up that attachment, he served a different master.[38] While Aristotle may not have taken such a strict view, by calling out the deficiency of stinginess he certainly argued for people to consider their own relationship to wealth.

Giving for human flourishing

Now we turn our attention to the potential and actual implications for the recipients of generosity. Cicero's "bounty is a bottomless pit" suggests that charitable giving creates a paternalistic connection that undermines a potentially healthy relationship, rendering the recipient as simply some object that needs money. Ethicist Lisa Cahill also supports that position, deeming the type of charitable giving that reinforces enablement and paternalistic relationships an "adverse virtue." She defines adverse virtue as a type of forced choice, constituting cooperation with a particular injustice responsible for the adversity in the first place.[39] Without realizing it, people often make choices in terms of giving money to others that ultimately have an adverse effect on the common good:

> Providing charity care is an expression of adverse virtue, in that it discerns as the best practical option a strategy that enables society

---

[36] Ulrich Luz, *Studies in Matthew* (Grand Rapids, Mich.: W.B. Eerdmans Publishing Company, 2005), 155.

[37] Luke 19:8 (Revised Standard Version).

[38] See also Matthew 6:24: "No one can serve two masters; for either he will hate the one and love the other, or he will be devoted to the one and despise the other. You cannot serve God and mammon" (Revised Standard Version).

[39] Lisa Sowle Cahill, *Theological Bioethics: Participation, Justice, and Change* (Washington, DC: Georgetown University Press, 2005), 119.

to escape responsibility and keeps the poor in a dependent, demeaning, and health-reducing situation. The provision of charity care is a moral obligation for religiously based health care services in view of the common good; yet it is also a form of cooperation in and even perpetuation of conditions detrimental to the common good.[40]

While Christ's words serve as an inspiration for his followers to give to others, both Aristotle and Cicero caution people to exercise prudence for the same reasons that Cahill so poignantly identifies. Charity might help as a temporary alleviation of pain and poverty, and in some cases, such as in fresh-disaster situations, it becomes absolutely necessary in the short term. But over the long term, institutionalized charity does little to help people help themselves. If eudaimonia is the ultimate driver, and furthermore cannot be given to someone, then any system set up to help the poor must include incentives for the recipients of generosity to flourish through their *own efforts*.

Child sponsorship

Some readers may recall watching commercials in the 1980s featuring television personality Sally Struthers pleading for viewers to give roughly seventy cents a day to sponsor a child through the Christian Children's Fund (now known as ChildFund International). The organization was originally established by a Presbyterian minister in 1938 to aid children displaced by the Sino-Japanese war. Over the years, ChildFund has slowly expanded its outreach to thirty countries, with the majority of their focus on Africa.

Under the child sponsorship model, donors contribute a set amount on a monthly basis that is directed to a specific child or community. Sponsors are encouraged to write letters and to send gifts to the child, sometimes receiving letters back from their sponsored child. To protect the safety of the children, all correspondence, gifts, and visits to the child are strictly regulated by organizational staff. Several organizations have replicated

---

[40] Cahill, *Theological Bioethics*, 149.

this model, including Save the Children, Plan International, and World Vision.

While these programs continue to help children and communities around the world, Researcher Erica Bornstein found that the child sponsorship program in Zimbabwe operated by the Christian organization World Vision shifted power dynamics within villages: "An irony of child sponsorship was that as much as child sponsorship linked people across nations in the transnational relationships of a global 'Christian family', it divided people locally and had an immense potential to inspire jealousy." She provides the example of a sponsor who paid for one child's education, but not for his siblings. This caused the sponsored child to become the object of jealousy which created tension between his Zimbabwean family and World Vision's staff.[41]

In addition to the high cost of running these programs, criticisms also include the paternalistic stance this model reinforces in both sponsors and communities. "Adopting a child" in a developing country can perpetuate negative stereotypes that citizens in those countries are helpless. It can also lead to confusion over the role of international aid in communities where members take little part in their own self-determination, cultivating relationships based on dependency.

One helpful structure can be drawn from the work of the medieval philosopher Maimonides, often considered the St. Thomas Aquinas of Judaism, who sketched eight levels of giving that serve as a useful guideline on giving for the sake of human flourishing. Although he framed these levels within the context of Jewish tradition, the model holds true for all human beings. His highest level of giving is to assist a person in becoming self-sufficient:

> The greatest level, above which there is no greater, is to support a fellow Jew by endowing him with a gift or loan, or entering into a partnership with him, or finding employment for him, in order

---

[41] Erica Bornstein, *The Spirit of Development: Protestant NGOs, Morality, and Economics in Zimbabwe* (Stanford, CA: Stanford University Press, 2005), 83–88.

to strengthen his hand until he need no longer be dependent upon others.[42]

This level of giving cultivates a partnership—a different kind of relationship than the type of paternalism that traditional charity often fosters, particularly in the form of a loan that is paid back. As this book will discuss in the discussion of usury in Chapter 5, early Jewish law forbade charging an interest rate on loans to other Jews. So presumably the highest level of giving calls for an *interest-free* loan. Ultimately, this interest-free loan avoids some of the detrimental effects to the common good because the partnership provides others with the opportunity to lift themselves out of poverty rather than keeping them in an impoverished, dependent state.

Maimonides: eight levels of charity

There are eight levels of charity, each greater than the next.

1. The greatest level, above which there is no greater, is to support a fellow Jew by endowing him with a gift or loan, or entering into a partnership with him, or finding employment for him, in order to strengthen his hand until he need no longer be dependent upon others...
2. A lesser level of charity than this is to give to the poor without knowing to whom one gives, and without the recipient knowing from who he received. For this is performing a mitzvah solely for the sake of Heaven. This is like the "anonymous fund" that was in the Holy Temple [in Jerusalem]. There the righteous gave in secret, and the good poor profited in secret. Giving to a charity fund is similar to this mode of charity, though one should not contribute to a charity fund unless one knows that the person appointed over the fund is trustworthy and wise and a proper administrator, like Rabbi Hananya ben Teradyon.

---

[42] Chabad.org, "Maimonides' Eight Levels of Charity," http://www.chabad.org/library/article_cdo/aid/45907/jewish/Eight-Levels-of-Charity.htm (accessed 31 December 2013).

3. A lesser level of charity than this is when one knows to whom one gives, but the recipient does not know his benefactor. The greatest sages used to walk about in secret and put coins in the doors of the poor. It is worthy and truly good to do this if those who are responsible for distributing charity are not trustworthy.
4. A lesser level of charity than this is when one does not know to whom one gives, but the poor person does know his benefactor. The greatest sages used to tie coins into their robes and throw them behind their backs, and the poor would come up and pick the coins out of their robes so that they would not be ashamed.
5. A lesser level than this is when one gives to the poor person directly into his hand, but gives before being asked.
6. A lesser level than this is when one gives to the poor person after being asked.
7. A lesser level than this is when one gives inadequately, but gives gladly and with a smile.
8. A lesser level than this is when one gives unwillingly.

Source: Mishneh Torah, Laws of Charity, 10, 7–14

Because it cultivates collaborative human relationships, this type of giving also promotes the kind of love mentioned earlier that passes through a person onto others, then back through God to complete the circuit.

Among the many different options for giving in the world, one has been gaining an increasing amount of exposure. Because of its promise to transform the lives of economically disadvantaged people, microfinance has become a practical option for supporting efforts to alleviate the effects of poverty. Maimonides's highest level of giving provides precisely the kind of inspiration that fuels microfinance efforts. To demonstrate this connection, the next chapter will introduce the world of microfinance, its historical roots, and the innovative ways that people and organizations, both faith and non-faith-based, have become involved in this highly effective way of helping the poor help themselves. The chapter will lay the groundwork for subsequent chapters that will focus on the role of faith in microfinance and other international development efforts.

2
Financial Services for Poverty Alleviation

"Give a man a fish, and he will eat for a day. Teach him how to fish, and he'll eat forever."[1]

Lao Tzu

This chapter will introduce the reader to the historical roots of the different forms of financial services directed toward the poor. These include various member-managed cooperative models, many of which have been created or inspired by faith-based organizations and other religiously affiliated advocates. The chapter also includes a section describing the ways that the poor themselves have developed simple but effective group models to access credit and to save money on their own. After an introduction to microcredit, the chapter will end with a discussion of microfinance, which seeks to integrate all of the various historical methods to create products and services that address the fundamental needs of the poor.

Cooperatives, credit unions, and Catholicism

In addition to producing satirical novels like *Gulliver's Travels*, the writer Jonathan Swift founded the first Irish Loan Fund in the 1720s. Starting with £500 in a revolving loan fund, Swift made small, uncollateralized loans to struggling tradesmen living in Dublin. As part of the credit approval process, each borrower had to obtain guarantees from two

---

[1] All Great Quotes, Lao Tzu, http://www.allgreatquotes.com/lao_tzu_quotes. shtml (accessed 31 December 2013).

neighbors. As Swift put it, this would ensure that the borrower was honest, sober, and industrious, rather than idle and dissolute.[2] By the mid-nineteenth century, the movement had grown to an estimated three hundred loan funds serving twenty percent of households throughout Ireland.[3] Some historians cite Swift as one of the progenitors of modern microcredit, which is an arguable distinction—but he certainly was among the first to employ a cooperative model to facilitate credit to families who, given their meager income levels and lack of sufficient collateral, could not access the formal banking sector on their own.

Both England and Germany also saw major shifts toward cooperative models in the mid-nineteenth century. These early associations relied upon three fundamental principles: self-help, self-administration, and self-responsibility.[4] These three principles have become integral to the survival and growth of cooperatives, credit unions, and other autonomous financial institutions wishing to remain independent of charity and political affiliation. Christian socialist cooperatives in Victorian England arose to provide a similar structure for people to help one another, since neither the state nor the market could, or would, supply the financial services that they wanted on acceptable terms.[5] In 1850, Herman Schulze, a German economist from Saxony, established the first thrift[6]-and-loan association for German craftsmen who had no access to the formal banking sector. This association still exists today as the modern Volksbank (German for "people's bank"), one of the largest financial conglomerates in the world. In 1862, German mayor Friedrich Wilhelm Raiffeisen founded the Heddesdorf Loan Society, a cooperative that helped poverty-stricken rural farmers to access credit through their own personal connections.[7] The cooperative

---

[2] Thomas Sheridan, *The Life of the Rev. Dr. Jonathan Swift,* 2nd ed. (London: Rivington, 1787), 234.

[3] Aidan Hollis, *Women and Microcredit in History, In Women and Credit: Researching the Past, Refiguring the Future* (New York: Berg, 2002), 74.

[4] German: *Selbsthilfe, Selbstverwaltung, and Selbstverantwortung.*

[5] Susan L. Buckley, *Teachings on Usury in Judaism, Christianity and Islam* (Lewiston, New York: The Edwin Mellen Press, 2000), 181.

[6] Thrifts are community-focused financial institutions that concentrate primarily on taking deposits and issuing low-cost mortgages.

[7] Die Genossenschaften, "Cooperatives in Germany: History of cooperatives," http://www.dgrv.de/en/cooperatives/historyofcooperatives.html (accessed 31 December 2013).

and its subsequent federations survive today as the powerful international Raiffeisen Banking Group.[8]

The late nineteenth and early twentieth centuries were the scene of burgeoning cooperative movements around the world, many inspired by religious voices advocating for financial inclusion of the poor. Pope Leo XIII's *Rerum Novarum* (Latin for "On the New Things"), an encyclical issued in 1891 and subtitled "Rights and Duties of Capital and Labor," argued for improving the lot of the working class. He particularly addressed the need for labor unions, striking an economic middle path by rejecting both socialism and unfettered capitalism (both were influential ideologies competing for primacy at the time), while affirming the need to maintain property rights for everyone.[9]

Rerum Novarum aimed to undercut the arguments of socialists, whose criticisms of the effects of industrialization and private property on European society were beginning to gain traction throughout the world. For example, the Socialist Labor Party of America was formed in 1876 and quickly garnered significant public support after federal troops intervened during a railroad strike in 1877 and 100 people wound up dead.[10] While sympathetic to the plight of the

---

[8] Raiffeisen Bank, "History of Raiffeisen Bank Group," http://www.raiffeisen.ru/en/about/bankgroup/ (accessed 31 December 2013).

[9] Leo XIII, Encyclical Letter, *Rerum Novarum* (of New Things), Vatican Website, 15 May 1891. http://www.vatican.va/holy_father/leo_xiii/encyclicals/documents/hf_l-xiii_enc_15051891_rerum-novarum_en.html (accessed 31 December 2013).

[10] The strike came about during the "Great Depression," as it was known before the 1930s—now referred to as the Great Panic of 1873 and ensuing "Long Depression." The causes of the economic downturn have been partially traced to post-Civil War inflation and Germany's decision to discontinue minting silver *thaler* coins (the English word *dollar* traces its origin from *thaler*) following the Franco-Prussian War (1870–1871). With silver prices dropping worldwide, the United States shifted its policy to a gold standard only (previously, it had backed both gold and silver, minting coins in both metals). This move led to a restriction in the money supply, raised interest rates, and caused a succession of bank failures at a time when Civil War reconstruction was losing financial and political steam, particularly in the railroad industry. The economy of the United States and other European nations suffered for several years, causing companies to close, labor strikes, and a general economic malaise. See Michael A. Bellesile's book *1877: America's Year of Living Violently* for more information about this period in US history.

working class who were being exploited by the industrialists, Pope Leo XIII cautioned against adopting an ideology he found too radical:

> To remedy these wrongs the socialists, working on the poor man's envy of the rich, are striving to do away with private property, and contend that individual possessions should become the common property of all, to be administered by the State or by municipal bodies. They hold that by thus transferring property from private individuals to the community, the present mischievous state of things will be set to rights, inasmuch as each citizen will then get his fair share of whatever there is to enjoy. But their contentions are so clearly powerless to end the controversy that were they carried into effect the working man himself would be among the first to suffer. They are, moreover, emphatically unjust, for they would rob the lawful possessor, distort the functions of the State, and create utter confusion in the community.[11]

Pope Leo XIII ultimately grounded his argument in the tenth commandment's admonition against coveting the possessions of one's neighbor.[12] For him, private property was a natural right that needed to be protected by the state.

In 1931, on the fortieth anniversary of *Rerum Novarum* and just as the Great Depression was gaining momentum, Pope Pius XI published the encyclical *Quadragesimo Anno* as an update on the struggle between unchecked capitalism and socialism.[13] Here Pope Pius XI introduced the term "social justice" to underscore the need to protect worker rights. While social charity focuses on those in a state of

---

[11] Leo XIII, *Rerum Novarum*, sec. 4.

[12] Leo XIII, *Rerum Novarum*, sec. 11.

[13] This actually began a pattern of papal encyclicals on similar topics: John XXIII's *Mater et Magistra* (1961), and John Paul II's *Centesimus Annus* (1991). John Paul II's encyclical focused on property rights and denouncing Marxism, which makes sense given the historical context of the recent collapse of the Soviet Union. This bears a sharp contrast to the lamentations of Pope Francis over social inequality and unfettered capitalism, referring to capitalism as "a new tyranny"—a position that has angered many conservative Catholics who had long grown comfortable with the Church's close-knit relationship and approval of capitalism in its many forms (see: http://www.vatican.va/holy_father/francesco/apost_exhortations/documents/papa-francesco_esortazione-ap_20131124_evangelii-gaudium_en.html).

abject poverty, social justice aims to protect workers from exploitation by ensuring a living wage and bringing free-market forces under
public control, where appropriate.[14] In order to delineate social
justice from socialism itself and avoid confusion between the terms,
Pope Pius XI made the unequivocal claim that "no one can be at the
same time a good Catholic and a true socialist."[15]

These encyclicals inspired Catholic Liberation Theology—the idea
that God, as theologian Fr. Gustavo Gutierrez put it, reserves a preferential option for the poor.[16] This means that while God's love extends
to all, God has revealed that the poor should come first. Liberation
Theology gained particular popularity in Latin America, and has
challenged both capitalism as an ideology and the Catholic Church's
relationship to that ideology. It has been seen as a direct response to
the Protestant Ethic (which will be covered in the next chapter) and
also a challenge to the Catholic Church's enthusiastic embracement
of capitalism. The Church eventually dismissed Liberation Theology
as too Marxist in its ideology—under Cardinal Ratzinger (who later
became Pope Benedict XVI)—deeming it a "fundamental threat to
the faith of the Church".[17] In Latin American and Africa it has since
competed with alternative movements such as the Prosperity Gospel.

Promoted by Evangelical Christians, the Prosperity Gospel argues
that God will deliver abundance *only* to the faithful and worthy. This
division persists even today, when travelers to Central America are
asked if they are either Christian or Catholic (an obvious backhanded
remark challenging the authenticity of Catholicism as a Christian
religion). The Prosperity Gospel and its influence and effects in Africa
will also be covered in Chapter 4 of this book.

The encyclicals also inspired the Catholic Distributist philosophy of the late nineteenth and early twentieth century—one that
advocates widespread property ownership among the working class.

---

[14] Pius XI, Encyclical Letter, *Quadragesimo Anno* (In the 40th Year), Vatican
Website, 15 May 1931, http://www.vatican.va/holy_father/pius_xi/encyc
licals/documents/hf_p-xi_enc_19310515_quadragesimo-anno_en.html,
sec. 110 (accessed 31 December 2013).

[15] Pius XI, *Quadragesimo Anno*, sec. 120.

[16] Gustavo Gutierrez, *A Theology of Liberation* (Maryknoll, New York: Orbison
Books, 2012).

[17] Joseph Cardinal Ratzinger, "Liberation Theology," From a private memo
published in the Italian press in 1984, http://www.christendom-awake.org/
pages/ratzinger/liberationtheol.htm (accessed 5 January 2014).

Seeking to subordinate economic activity to one's spiritual or family life, it gained traction as influential writers such as G. K. Chesterton began promoting it as a counter to both socialism and capitalism. Distributist thought influenced other Catholic causes, such as the Catholic Worker Movement founded by Dorothy Day and Peter Maurin in New York City in 1933. With over one hundred communities still operating around the world today, the Catholic Worker Movement provides social services to those living on the margins of society. Through its newspaper, *The Catholic Worker*, the movement has served as a staunch voice of pacifism and advocate for the redistribution of wealth as it seeks to "live in accordance with the justice and charity of Jesus Christ."[18] Dorothy Day, who is currently being considered for Catholic sainthood, deplored the concept of lending money at interest. In fact, she once returned a check for several thousand dollars to the City of New York Treasurer's office; the check represented the interest the city paid on an overdue debt owed to The Catholic Worker. In her written response, she derides the entire "system" of profit making, citing Matthew 25 (the Parable of the Talents, in which a servant is punished for hoarding wealth).[19] In keeping with its principles of solidarity and protecting the rights of workers, the Catholic Worker Movement has been a strong proponent of credit unions as an alternative to the traditional banking system.

The Antigonish Movement, started in Nova Scotia in the 1930s and since spread to other eastern Canadian Maritime[20] provinces, is a prime example of a collective movement inspired by the papal encyclicals. Dr Moses Coady and two other Catholic priests who studied in Rome during the papacy of Pope Pius XI brought those ideas back with them to Antigonish, Nova Scotia to address the social and economic problems of the community and region.[21]

---

[18] The Catholic Worker Movement, "The Aims and Means of the Catholic Worker," http://www.catholicworker.org/aimsandmeanstext.cfm?Number=5 (accessed 31 December 2013).

[19] The Catholic Worker Movement, "This Money is not Ours" by Dorothy Day, http://www.catholicworker.org/DorothyDay/daytext.cfm?TextID=768, 6 September 1960 (accessed 31 December 2013).

[20] A region of Eastern Canada consisting of three provinces, New Brunswick, Nova Scotia, and Prince Edward Island.

[21] Anne Alexander, *The Antigonish Movement: Moses Coady and Adult Education Today* (Toronto: Thompson Educational Publishing, Inc., 1997), 71.

Since the settling of Canada, the Maritimes had enjoyed some level of prosperity in the fishing industry; during the nineteenth century, they experienced this in manufacturing as well. As historian Anne Alexander has argued, the Maritimes' slow and steady economic decline in the early twentieth century can be partially attributed to deindustrialization and to shifting national economic policies that eroded the region's competitive advantage.[22] The Maritime Rights Movement of the 1920s brought together workers, industrialists, clergy, and academics in an attempt to protect the Maritimes. In response to this and other movements—including persistent coal miner strikes that ended in violence and death—Prime Minister Mackenzie King reduced freight rates and increased subsidies in 1926 to "defuse the Maritime agitation."[23] These and other attempts to influence national legislation through local labor parties such as the United Farmers of Nova Scotia and the Nova Scotia Labour Party did little to thwart the downward spiral. However, the "drive to reform remained and showed its expression in the development of cooperatives."[24]

Based out of St. Francis Xavier University in Antigonish, Nova Scotia, Dr Moses Coady helped organize these struggling fishermen and farmers into small meetings called "study clubs," where workers would discuss ways to stem the tide of people leaving rural areas to search for work in larger cities—primarily outside the Maritimes. The Antigonish Movement, as it later became known, sought the "improvement of the economic, social educational, and religious condition of the people of eastern Nova Scotia."[25] Ultimately, the movement spread across the Maritimes with its fundamental philosophy that "through education and economic cooperation people could enhance their own lives and create a more humane society."[26] With adult education central to the Antigonish Movement's philosophy, the University established the Extension Department in 1933, headed by Coady, to train the leaders of the study clubs and the cooperatives that began springing up.[27] Coady was instrumental

---

[22] Alexander, *The Antigonish Movement*, 9.

[23] Alexander, *The Antigonish Movement*, 32.

[24] Alexander, *The Antigonish Movement*, 33.

[25] The Cooperative League, *How St. Francis Xavier University Educates for Action*, 48. Cited in Alexander, *The Antigonish Movement*, 78.

[26] Alexander, *The Antigonish Movement*, 78.

[27] Alexander, *The Antigonish Movement*, 81.

in establishing the first credit union in English-speaking Canada in 1932, with 142 credit unions quickly spreading across Nova Scotia within five years' time.[28]

Coady and the Antigonish Movement's focus on adult education had an enormous influence on the development of credit unions across Canada. Vancouver City Savings Credit Union (VanCity), boasting over 400,000 members and Canada's largest credit union in terms of assets, continues to host a wide variety of financial literacy courses for its members—with some curricula designed specifically for Aboriginal youth and adults.[29] In 1959, St. Francis Xavier University opened the Coady International Institute as the main vehicle for spreading the Antigonish Movement internationally.[30] The Coady Institute continues to offer education grounded in the Antigonish Movement philosophy of community-based development. Its courses and diploma programs attract community leaders from around the world, with an increased emphasis on microfinance as a tool for community-driven development.[31]

The poor and their money

Although cooperatives and credit unions have experienced tremendous success in developed countries, developing countries historically have not been able to afford the overhead required to scale them for the poor. In the absence of these services, the poor have developed methods to acquire and manage money on their own—and sometimes with the help of development organizations working on the ground. Some of the ideas and lessons learned from these approaches have helped to create more robust and effective models used in microfinance that address the fundamental fiduciary needs of the poor. Because microfinance has been so heavily influenced by

[28] Alexander, *The Antigonish Movement*, 88.
[29] Vancouver City Savings Credit Union, "Financial literacy and basic banking," https://www.vancity.com/AboutVancity/VisionAndValues/ValuesBasedBanking/FinancialLiteracyAndBasicBanking/ (accessed 31 December 2013).
[30] Coady International Institute, Masters of Their Own Destiny: The Coady Story in Canada and Across the World, "The Antigonish Movement," http://coadyextension.stfx.ca/antigonish-movement/ (accessed 31 December 2013).
[31] Coady International Institute, "Transformative Leadership Education Programs," http://coady.stfx.ca/education/ (accessed 31 December 2013).

these methods that its very existence as a refined version of micro-credit might not have been possible without them, it is important to examine those methods in detail.

Like everyone else, poor people also need the ability to raise lump sums of cash for life-cycle needs (e.g. births, deaths, and marriages), for seizing business and investment opportunities, or to pay for other expected and unexpected large expenses.[32] Aside from selling or pawning one's possessions, the main options available are *saving up, saving down (loans), or saving through*.[33] The next three sections will explore each of these three options and how the poor have managed their money *without the help of formal financial institutions*. A majority of the material found in these three sections is taken from Stuart Rutherford's accessible and groundbreaking book *The Poor and Their Money*, considered a foundational text for microfinance and development practitioners. While the following three sections provide a brief overview, readers wanting a deeper understanding of the material are encouraged to pick up a copy of the book.

Saving up

When it comes to saving money, the main challenge people face in developing countries is not a lack of motivation or discipline, but finding a safe place to store their money.[34] In fact, this issue has long historical roots. Before the invention of hard currency, in most early societies commodities such as barley were stored in huge containers inside temples (generally the most secure place in the community) and used for payment against credit charges. The value of barley was normally fixed to a precious metal such as silver. This type of system

---

[32] Stuart Rutherford, *The Poor and their Money* (New Delhi: Oxford University Press, 2000), 4.
[33] Stuart Rutherford, a microfinance practitioner and author of the influential book *The Poor and Their Money*, coined the term "saving through" to encompass a broad spectrum of ways to receive money at an intermediate point in time while making a more or less continuous savings. See Rutherford, *The Poor and their Money*, 8.
[34] Although, the authors of the book *Poor Economics*, who based their research on years of working with clients, make the claim that poor people value savings tools as a way to keep the money safe from other members of the household (and even themselves). See Abhijit V. Banerjee and Esther Duflo, *Poor Economics* (New York: Public Affairs, 2001), 196.

was so common that in his book *Debt: the First 5,000 Years*, scholar David Graeber debunks the myth that barter was in widespread use before the discovery of money. He lays out a plausible argument that barter was in fact rarely—if ever—employed in any society, despite still being touted by most economists as the precursor to coinage.[35] Grain banks and other forms of credit were used most often in lieu of tangible currency.

Because barley and other commodities were perishable and subject to spoilage and bug infestation, currency slowly evolved to include items such as shells and beads and eventually coins made of precious metals. Finally, paper money came into circulation as a more portable way to carry currency and to conduct transactions—backed by precious metals and other assets, legally enforceable promises, and as is more common today, the economic stability of the issuer of the note (generally a nation state).[36] Over time, banks replaced temples as the safe houses for storing precious metals and other forms of currency. However, today banks still remain out of reach for the world's poorest, whose small savings fail to meet minimum thresholds for deposit.

To fill this gap, some trusted people in some poor communities work as deposit collectors. Rutherford captures the demand for this role when he says, "The need to find a safe place to keep savings is so strong that some poor people willingly pay others to take their savings out of their hands and store them."[37] Clients who use these services pay the deposit collector a set amount on a regularly agreed upon basis (often daily), and at the end of an agreed upon period, receive their savings in a lump-sum minus a small fee for service.[38]

---

[35] David Graeber, *Debt: The First 5,000 Years* (New York: Melville House Publishing, 2011), 40–41.

[36] It will be interesting to learn how long paper money itself remains a standard as world societies begin shifting more and more towards electronic and other cashless transactions.

[37] Rutherford, *The Poor and Their Money*, 13.

[38] For more information, please read the following articles: http://dailyinde pendentnig.com/2012/11/no-comets-for-a-pioneer/ (accessed 5 January 2014) and http://www.punchng.com/feature/baba-alajo-somolu-a-legend-dies-unsung/ (accessed 5 January 2014).

As Rutherford points out, clients are willing to accept a negative interest rate on savings due to a lack of supply of savings services.[39] In India, some clients can only afford to deposit five rupees a day (roughly eleven cents), an amount even the smallest banks would hesitate to accept. Furthermore, clients often commit to schedules with a predetermined savings goal; these schedules may be dictated by needs such as an upcoming school fees payment or other family event such as a wedding or a birth. Clients use deposit collectors to ensure that they can successfully save up for something without the risk of losing those savings by storing them under a mattress or in a hole in the floor, then losing them through misplacement or theft. As long as poor people, particularly those living in remote areas, remain outside the reach of banks, deposit collectors will continue to fill the demand for finding a safe place to store savings.

Saving down

Historically, poor people often resort to local moneylenders who charge exorbitant interest rates and employ aggressive collection methods such as leg breaking and other forms of physical and psychological pressure. However, according to Rutherford, the most frequent problem poor people face comes not from the price of loans, but in persuading moneylenders to give them an advance in the first place.[40] In small rural communities, moneylenders often base their lending decisions on first-hand knowledge of the borrower's trustworthiness and reputation— information commercial banks do not have the resources to obtain.[41]

Many moneylenders will charge clients who lack collateral an upfront fee rather than include interest into the repayment schedule. For example, a 5,000 Mexican Peso (MXN) loan might have 1,000 MXN held back by the moneylender. The borrower receives 4,000 MXN up front, but is on the hook for the 5,000 MXN loan, paid back over regular weekly intervals. Because the payout comes first, and can be understood as an *advance against future savings*, Rutherford calls this *saving down* as opposed to *saving up*. Ultimately, this form of "savings" is more costly to poor people because the moneylender factors the higher risk level into the loan.

---

[39] Rutherford, *The Poor and Their Money*, 15.
[40] Rutherford, *The Poor and Their Money*, 93.
[41] Rutherford, *The Poor and Their Money*, 19.

Saving through

Those outside of the formal banking sector have developed innovative, homegrown ways both to save together and to make loans to one another without the need for either deposit collectors or money-lenders. The two primary models in use are the Rotating Savings and Credit Association (ROSCA) and the Accumulating Savings and Credit Association (ASCA). These savings clubs, as they are often called, each carry benefits and drawbacks that will be explored in this section.

Sometimes called a merry-go-round fund, the basic principle of the ROSCA is that members make fixed contributions at fixed intervals (daily, weekly, or monthly), with each member receiving a lump sum based on a predetermined ordering system. For example, suppose a group of ten people in Manila decide to create a ROSCA and agree to contribute 200 Philippine Pesos (PhP) weekly. Each member is assigned a number from one to ten (through vote, lottery, or some other form of mutual agreement). At the end of the first week, the members meet and each contributes 200 PhP, with one member receiving the pot of 2,000 PhP. The same pattern is repeated the following week, with the member second in rotation receiving the 2,000 PhP lump sum, and so forth. After ten weeks the members can start the process all over again (with or without modifying membership or ordering) or they can simply dissolve the group.

As self-selective groups, trust is an obvious key component in the ROSCA's effectiveness. Members often know one another quite well, either through family or through community connections. Some ROSCAs start out with a small membership base and slowly grow in size as new members are added over time (To manage risk, new members are often the last in order to receive their lump sum). Many well-functioning ROSCA groups last for several years, repeating the cycles over and over again.

The precise origin of the ROSCA model remains a mystery, and a 1956 paper by renowned anthropologist Clifford Geertz entitled "The Rotating Credit Association: A 'Middle Rung' in Development" argues that the ROSCA model is "a product of a shift from a traditionalistic agrarian society to an increasingly fluid commercial one."[42]

---

[42] Clifford Geertz, "The Rotating Credit Association: A Middle Rung in Development," http://hypergeertz.jku.at/GeertzTexts/Rotating_Credit1.htm (accessed 31 December 2013).

Geertz found striking similarities in homegrown ROSCA models in Java, China, Japan, Vietnam, West Africa, the Caribbean, and in the southern United States. This suggests that perhaps ROSCAs were not taught from the outside, but rather emerged organically based on societal needs. ROSCAs can be found all over the world, each taking on a local name—with the *susu* in Ghana being one of the most well known (derived from the Yoruba word *esusu*, meaning "pooling the funds").

As savings vehicles, ROSCAs can be very efficient and effective at building trust without the need for middlemen or outside parties. However, they carry some limitations. The first is that they rely heavily on an expectation that members will be able to make their fixed contribution consistently and on schedule. All it takes is for one member to fall on hard times to disrupt the entire system. The other prime limitation is that ROSCAs deny members access either to loans or to the ability to earn interest on their savings.

To address some of the limitations of the ROSCA model, economic development practitioners created the ASCA as a means for people to accumulate savings and to make loans to members. ASCAs can be time-bound (usually lasting twelve months) or open-ended, with variations on the model throughout the world. The basic principle is that self-selecting members meet on a regular basis, normally weekly, to make a fixed deposit. Each deposit is recorded into a simple ledger book and also into member passbooks. In communities with low literacy levels, the passbook record is often recorded as a stamp representing a specific amount. Members can then make an additional deposit on top of the requirement, and would then receive extra stamps in their passbooks. Failure to pay the required deposit often results in an additional penalty payment due at the next meeting, along with any delinquent deposit amounts. Members can take on loans as well, paying back with interest.

Given that this model seeks to accumulate savings, collected savings need to be protected. In rural communities this can often present a distinct challenge given the lack of safe places to store money. Nevertheless, the most prevalent method has been to use a strongbox made of either steel or hardwood, secured by three padlocks. At the end of each meeting, the keys to each padlock are disbursed to members on a rotating and/or random basis. The box itself is stored at the home of the treasurer, the most trusted person in the group with the most secure place to store the box between meetings. The risks of the treasurer running off with the box or colluding with other members is somewhat mitigated by social pressures, which often carry enough power to insulate the group from this danger.[43]

As mentioned earlier, some members may take out interest-bearing loans against the group's deposited funds. These can be for business or consumption needs. The interest itself can be quite high (e.g. a flat 1% per week, amounting to an annual percentage rate of 52%). This grows the pot of funds much more quickly and rewards savers over the long term, since profits generated by the interest payments are shared by members either when the ASCA completes its cycle or periodically if the ASCA is not time-bound. The deposit stamps in the passbook are counted and the funds divided among members on that basis, taking into account any outstanding loans. Ultimately, those with the most stamps stand to gain the most, providing an incentive to become a consistent saver rather than a habitual borrower.

One of the ASCA model's greatest achievements is people learning to come together to manage wealth and to direct it in ways that help one another and the communities where they live. Meetings also serve as venues to discuss issues important to the community such as personal safety, health, and sanitation. ASCAs are often formed through strong social or religious connections, with meetings beginning with a prayer or another ritual to bring people together in community. For this reason, these clubs are a natural means for members to express solidarity through additional loans to handle emergencies (often interest-free). This provides a safety valve to members who suffer extreme circumstances such as a medical or family emergency. Some clubs also choose to pool together deposits for joint business ventures or to fund community projects. Run successfully, an ASCA group can become a very powerful force and voice in the community.

The ASCA model is a highly effective tool for the poor to manage credit and savings on their own. However, it does require training and oversight, which is often best performed through development organizations that can work directly with the communities. Catholic Relief Services (CRS) has pioneered a successful version in Africa

---

[43] With the increased usage of mobile and electronic monetary transaction services throughout the world, the physical box structure is slowly being replaced by these technologies, particularly in urban areas.

through its Savings and Internal Lending Club (SILC) model developed by Guy Vanmeenen.[44] Using its channels through Catholic churches, CRS trains local people as field agents who can spread this model in communities. These field agents provide upfront training and regular oversight for each club to ensure that rules are properly established and followed. The training consists of teaching members how to record transactions and to handle money in a way that provides for an open and transparent environment.

All of the materials, including the box, locks, and books, are provided upfront and then paid back by the group once a critical mass in savings has been accumulated. This pay-for-service model is crucial to ensure that the program is self-supporting and can be expanded to other communities. It also defines a relationship with communities that moves away from a dependency mindset and toward one where recipients have a stake in making things work. While field agents are paid by CRS, models offered by other organizations may or may not require field-agent support to be paid by the ASCA itself.[45] In order to completely move away from charity and its sociological and psychological effects, ASCA promoters should consider models that recover *all costs* from members.[46]

Origins of modern microcredit

In the 1970s, Dr Muhammad Yunus, a Vanderbilt-trained economist and head of the economics department at Chittagong University

---

[44] Savings-Revolution.org, "Online Savings-led Library," http://savings-revolution.org/doclib/Savings%20and%20Internal%20Lending%20Communities%20SILC%20a%20Basis%20for%20Integral%20Human%20Development.pdf (accessed 2 January 2014).

[45] Four international NGOs (Oxfam, CARE, CRS, and PACT,) have created the Access2Finance (A2F) consortium in Phnom Penh, Cambodia to share best practices in savings-led microfinance. For more information, see http://issuu.com/access2finance#!

[46] In 2008, Catholic Relief Services received a USD $8M grant from the Gates Foundation to support its SILC program in East Africa (See http://crs.org/newsroom/releases/release.cfm?id=1562). While this has allowed the organization to spread the program, it ultimately establishes a standard that ASCAs need to be supported by foundational dollars. It also reduces the incentive to develop ways to make those programs entirely self-supporting and ultimately sustainable in the long run.

in Bangladesh, realized that the trickle-down economics he taught in the classroom was not reaching the very poor.[47] In his autobiography, *Banker to the Poor*, he recounts a conversation he had with a rural villager in 1976:

"Do you own this bamboo?" I asked.

"Yes."

"How do you get it?"

"I buy it."

"How much does the bamboo cost you?"

"Five taka." At the time this was about twenty-two cents.

"Do you have five taka?"

"No, I borrow it from the *paikars*."

"From the middlemen? What is your arrangement with them?"

"I must sell my bamboo stools back to them at the end of the day as repayment for my loan."

"How much do you sell a stool for?"

"Five taka and fifty poysha."

"So you make fifty poysha profit?"

She nodded. That came to a profit of just two cents.

"And could you borrow the cash from the moneylender and buy your own raw material?"

"Yes, but the moneylender would demand a lot. People who deal with them only get poorer."

"How much does the moneylender charge?"

"It depends. Sometimes he charges 10 percent per week. But I have one neighbor who is paying 10 percent per day."

"And this is all you earn from making these beautiful bamboo stools, fifty poysha?"

"Yes."[48]

The obvious exploitation in the story prompted Yunus to loan the woman and forty-one other members of her village a total of 856 taka (less than USD $27)—and thus the Grameen Bank was born.[49] Gradually, he refined a loan process that relied heavily on state

---

[47] Muhammad Yunus, *Banker to the Poor* (New York: Public Affairs, 2003), 34.

[48] Yunus, *Banker to the Poor*, 47.

[49] Yunus, *Banker to the Poor*, 49.

grants and donor funds, developing what has come to be known as the *Grameen Method* of microcredit lending. He named the bank Grameen after the Bengali word that literally means "concerning villages."

As the historical accounts in the previous sections illustrated, loaning money to poor people is not particularly innovative, but Yunus's original approach included a fundamental component that resolved the difficulty of extending uncollateralized loans. Individuals did not receive loans unless they formed a peer-lending group composed of five people. Once they came together, the Grameen Bank extended a loan to two members of the group. If these two repaid regularly for the next six weeks, two additional members could request loans, with the chairperson being the last in the group to receive a loan. If an individual in that group was unable or unwilling to pay back his or her loan, other members were not required to cover the loan, but the group would then become ineligible for additional loans until it brought the repayment problem under control. This created a powerful incentive for borrowers to help one another not only to solve financial problems, but also to *prevent* problems. Essentially, the members of the peer-lending group served as an alternative form of collateral for one another rather than as outside guarantors.[50]

Using its microcredit strategy, the Grameen Bank has addressed the challenges of poverty to help close to fifty million people,[51] despite the cynicism of skeptics who originally suggested that it would never work. In his book, Yunus makes a compelling argument: "The poor, once economically empowered, are the most determined fighters in the battle to solve the population problem, end illiteracy, and live

---

[50] Yunus, *Banker to the Poor*, 62–66. Note: this model is based on the "Classic Grameen" model, which has since been revised such that joint liability of the group for the loan taken by one member (making members responsible for one another's loans) has been removed (See Grameen II for more information: Grameen Bank, "Grameen II," http://www.grameen-info.org/index.php?option=com_content&task=view&id=30&Itemid=116 (accessed 31 December 2013). One contributing factor for moving away from this model was that in several cases, group members applied direct pressure on delinquent members that resembled collection practices used by unsavory moneylenders.

[51] Grameen Bank, "Grameen Bank at a Glance," http://www.grameen-info.org/index.php?option=com_content&task=view&id=26&Itemid=0 (accessed 31 December 2013.

healthier, better lives. When policymakers finally realize that the poor are their partners, rather than bystanders or enemies, we will progress much faster than we do today."[52] The success of microcredit lies in the collaborative relationships that it fosters with the poor, rather than the paternalism inherent in traditional charity. With its innovative group-lending model, the Grameen Bank has attracted so many clients and donors that as of October 2011, they had dispersed USD $11.35 billion in loans since the bank's inception in 1976.[53] In December 2006, the Grameen Bank also won the Nobel Peace Prize "for their efforts to create economic and social development from below."[54]

Who really "founded" microcredit?

Muhammad Yunus has long been considered the "father" of microcredit, certainly reinforced by winning the Nobel Peace Prize. However, during the 1970s and prior to the establishment of the Grameen Bank, two other organizations were engaging in microloans separately in other parts of the world.

ACCION (Taking its name for the Spanish word "Action"), now based in Boston, Massachusetts originally started in 1961 as a grass roots community development initiative to help poor people in Venezuela but slowly branching out across Latin America. Through one of its affiliate members, it began offering loans to what it called "microenterprises" in the small town of Recife, Brazil in 1973. Within four years they had provided 885 loans to the poor in Recife.[55] Since then, ACCION has grown its worldwide network of 63 affiliate partners covering 32 countries in Latin America, Africa, Asia, and even the United States.[56]

In 1974, The Self Employment Women's Association (SEWA), a trade union in Gujarat (Western India), created SEWA Bank in

---

[52] Yunus, *Banker to the Poor,* 137.
[53] Grameen Bank, "Grameen Bank at a Glance."
[54] Nobelprize.org, "The Nobel Peace Prize 2006," http://nobelprize.org/nobel_prizes/peace/laureates/2006/ (accessed 31 December 2013).
[55] ACCION, "Our History," http://www.accion.org/about-us/history/1970s (accessed 31 December 2013).
[56] ACCION, "About Us," http://www.accion.org/about-us (accessed 31 December 2013).

order to serve women in the surrounding community with access to both credit and savings.[57] It holds the recognition of being the first microfinance bank, and has since grown to a net worth of nearly USD $40 million.[58] In addition to savings and loans, SEWA provides robust financial literacy and business counseling programs to women.

The promise of helping the poor through microcredit has attracted faith-based organizations that bring many built-in advantages, including affiliate networks and the ability to tap donor capital even in times of economic uncertainty. The story of CRS and its foray into microcredit apart from its work in ASCA savings clubs illustrates the challenges of faith-based organizations directly engaging in money lending and trying to balance a double-bottom line of fiscal and social performance. The international humanitarian agency of the Catholic community in the United States, CRS was founded in 1943 by the Catholic Bishops of the United States to serve World War II survivors in Europe. With a focus on poverty alleviation through public policy advocacy and a wide range of international development programs, CRS has served more than one hundred million people in more than 100 countries on five continents.[59] In 1989, CRS decided that microcredit would allow them to tap into their vast network of grassroots partners in order to bring financial services to the rural poor.[60]

Starting with a grant of $25,000, by 2005 CRS had a loan portfolio of $19 million and operations in 21 countries.[61] The impressive numbers, however, concealed deep rifts that threatened to tear the agency apart. As Kim Wilson, former senior advisor to CRS, puts it, "One part of the agency was intent on building sustainable businesses

---

[57] Shri Mahila Sewa Sahakari Bank Ltd., "History," http://www.sewabank. com/history.html (accessed 2 January 2014).

[58] Shri Mahila Sewa Sahakari Bank Ltd., "Latest News," http://www.sewabank. com/news-events.html (accessed 2 January 2014).

[59] Catholic Relief Services, "About Catholic Relief Services," http://www. catholicrelief.org/about/ (accessed 2 January 2014).

[60] Kim Wilson, "The Moneylender's Dilemma," in *What's Wrong with Microfinance?* ed. by Thomas Dichter and Malcolm Harper (Warwickshire, UK: Practical Action Publishing, 1997), 98.

[61] Wilson, "The Moneylender's Dilemma," 99.

or helping partners to build them, and all other parts were seeking to deliver humanitarian or development services. Barriers between microfinance and other sectors rose, threatening a kind of balkanization that seemed less like healthy rivalry and more like a cold war."[62]

For some at CRS, building a sustainable program meant providing heavy investment and competing in the marketplace in terms of interest rates. CRS's competitive market rates were often as high as eighty-seven percent per year and their operations required a substantial investment—from $150 to $300 per client. Aside from the microcredit operations becoming a financial sinkhole, CRS realized that they had become merely a subsidized moneylender.[63] Wilson underscores the extent to which CRS drifted away from its mission of helping the poor:

> Best practices implied that an organization must mine each customer for enough debt to contribute to the profitability of the MFI [microfinance institution]. Our MFIs required continued flows of revenue from repeat customers to stay in business. "I wanted to stop after three loan cycles", said one borrower in Nicaragua, "but the loan officer told me that I could never get another loan if I stopped." ... Tracking down delinquents (often referred to as deadbeats), which is the stock-in-trade of a good moneylender, was taking a toll ... Staff wanted to be the champion of a community, yet found it against their self-interest. Collecting late loan payments could further rupture relations ... One loan officer was so upset about confronting late borrowers that she confided in tears that she wanted another job. "They do not see me as helping them, but as an enemy." Pressured loan tactics took other forms as well. Take the example of the priest who announced the names of tardy borrowers at the end of Mass.[64]

Furthermore, CRS initially offered a group savings fund that slowly began to compete with the loan program. The risk of clients turning to their savings rather than taking on additional debt posed too great a threat to the program's self-sufficiency, so the

---

[62] Wilson, "The Moneylender's Dilemma," 100.
[63] Wilson, "The Moneylender's Dilemma," 101.
[64] Wilson, "The Moneylender's Dilemma," 103–104.

organization dismantled the groups saving fund.[65] The reliance on perpetual debt cycles remains the Achilles Heel of group-lending models, where borrowers feel obliged to keep taking on loans just to remain in a group. This is something that the ASCA model resolves as member choices between savings and loans do not threaten their membership in the group. Faced with a dilemma between serving communities and losing their trust, CRS decided in 2005 to divest its holdings in microcredit in favor of savings-led microfinance. Wilson outlines their reasoning for the sudden switch to broader microfinance services:

> Our efforts would focus on neglected rural areas where savings was a priority and on legal protection and remedy where we had the capacity to effect change. We would be free to link clients to resources (banks, post-offices or microfinance institutions) and champion their rights with regard to these resources. This would align us with the Catholic Social Teaching principle of Right Relationships. We would shift private funds away from microcredit and toward education, community development and emergency relief. We could go back to the real work of charity and see poor people as partners in a shared liberation, and not as experiments in quasi-commerce. Our dilemmas as moneylenders could at last become history.[66]

CRS discovered the potential risks associated with faith-based money lending, evoking the admonition from the Gospel of Matthew: "No one can serve two masters ... You cannot serve both God and money."[67] Furthermore, as benefactors who traditionally engage in charity (something particularly acute in the Catholic context), direct lending by faith-based organizations often confuses poor people who are already accustomed to receiving free money and services from them. Nevertheless, CRS succeeded in redefining its relationships to its clients because it holds itself accountable to both its mission and to the people it aims to help.

---

[65] Wilson, "The Moneylender's Dilemma," 104.
[66] Wilson, "The Moneylender's Dilemma," 107.
[67] Matthew 6:24 (Revised Standard Version).

The CRS case also reinforces the argument that credit alone is not enough to bring meaningful change to communities.[68] Proponents of loan-centric models cite data showing high demand for loans as proof for their necessity.[69] Indeed, it would be difficult to argue that strictly savings-based programs would be enough for poor people to pull themselves out of poverty. Nevertheless, the high demand for loans does not necessarily mean that the lives of clients are improving. In fact, spiraling indebtedness may be why they keep coming back for more loans.[70]

Over the past four decades, the Grameen Bank and other international development organizations have recognized that providing additional financial services is a highly effective way to help the poor. In the early years of microcredit, many people took out loans to fund their small businesses. Increasingly, the poor needed money for a variety of fiduciary issues, including medical payments and school tuition. Earlier sections demonstrated that savings-led programs found in ROSCAs and ASCAs prove that the poor are also capable of self-management and that credit alone is not enough to address their fiduciary needs. The next section will examine how organizations are integrating all of the available financial tools to further address the fundamental needs of the poor.

Microfinance: beyond microcredit

Modern microfinance has drawn upon several hundred years of credit union and cooperative systems, incorporating their focus on self-help, self-administration, and self-responsibility. Today, some ten thousand microfinance institutions operate in countries throughout the world—and most offer more than small business loans.

---

[68] Beatriz Armendariz de Aghion and Jonathan Morduch, *The Economics of Microfinance* (Cambridge, MA: MIT Press, 2005), 193.

[69] Syed Hashemi, "Beyond Good Intentions: Measuring Social Performance of Microfinance Institutions," CGAP Focus Note No. 41 (Washington DC: The World Bank, May 2007), 2.

[70] The Microfinance Gateway, "The Debate About Social Performance," http://www.microfinancegateway.org/resource_centers/socialperformance/today (accessed 1 January 2014. Hashemi also argues that high demand for loans does not automatically imply that people's conditions are improving (See: Hashemi, "Beyond Good Intentions," 2).

Microcredit is still the primary focus of microfinance institutions, but most organizations also engage in activities such as deposit savings, life insurance, medical insurance, loan insurance, education loans, home-improvement loans, pensions, scholarships, job training, and handling remittances sent by family members working abroad.[71] The additional services, particularly savings, are vital components to helping the poor become financially stable.

Both microcredit and microfinance should be seen as tools for relatively effective poverty *alleviation*—not *eradication*. Muhammad Yunus is often quoted as saying that one day people will visit poverty museums. While this may indeed be true someday, the world has an enormous amount of work to do in order to get to that point—and microfinance alone is not going to get us there. In his book *The Bottom Billion*, Oxford professor Paul Collier sketches out four broad reasons detailing why some countries still remain impoverished despite a tremendous amount of international aid and attention. As Collier puts it, these countries are caught in development traps due to poor governance, close proximity to unstable countries, internal conflict and civil war, and issues related to natural resources.[72] These development traps often trace their roots to greed, corruption, and other social ailments triggered through actions by selfish individuals. While microfinance can indeed help to channel vital financial resources to alleviate the effects of poverty, just like anything else it cannot serve as a panacea to cure all ailments related to poverty. The uphill battle faced by the poor living in particularly violent and unstable environments suggests that the words of one ancient Chinese philosopher still lay at the root of many societal problems: "If there is to be peace in the world ... there must first be peace in the heart."[73]

Nevertheless, one of the strongest arguments for continuing the mission of microfinance comes out of the financial-diaries work found in the book *Portfolios of the Poor*. The author interviewed poor households twice a month in Bangladesh, India, and South Africa over the course of a year. These interviews were designed to investigate how these households manage their money, and from

---

[71] Armendariz de Aghion and Morduch, *The Economics of Microfinance*, 14.

[72] Paul Collier, *The Bottom Billion: Why the Poorest Countries are Failing and What Can Be Done About It* (New York: Oxford University Press, 2007).

[73] Attributed to Lao Tzu (570–490 BCE).

this research the interviewers were able to construct 250 financial "diaries."[74] These diaries cover not only the management of household income, but also how the family handles the kinds of fixed and variable expenses that arise. In analyzing the collected diaries, the authors uncovered three primary needs that drive much of the financial behavior of the poor households they interviewed.

First, most of the households live on less than $2 a day—but this does not mean that they consistently earn two dollars each and every day. Highly irregular and sometimes unpredictable income flows make managing that income a crucial part for survival. In short, out of necessity, poor households are often extremely effective at managing cash flows. Nevertheless, what they desire are ways to help smooth those income flows to meet their daily needs and to plan for the future. This is simply not feasible if one does not adequately know when money will next come into the household.[75]

The second need relates to the first. Irregular income streams can render it nearly impossible to deal with household emergencies without some reserve, or access to immediate cash or credit. Many poor people wind up indebted to loan sharks when faced with medical emergencies that require a cash-only transaction to a hospital that may mean life or death for a family member. The developed world has various forms of credit, or even free national health care options, that are either unavailable to or extremely limited for many poor households. More importantly, this underscores the need to provide the poor with a range of insurance options, rather than simply access to debt.[76]

Lastly, the financial diarists uncovered the need for the poor to raise lump sums of cash in order to seize opportunities and to pay for big-ticket expenses. As the authors point out, loans can act as "accelerators," and the quickest way for the poor to achieve the lump-sum amount they desire.[77] Of course, this often comes at a higher price than if they were to join a ROSCA or an ASCA group. Sometimes, however, this is not possible due to timing of extraordinary events or the unavailability of groups where people could save together.

---

[74] Daryl Collins et al., *Portfolios of the Poor* (Princeton, New Jersey: Princeton University Press, 2009), 4.

[75] Collins, *Portfolios of the Poor*, 17.

[76] Collins, *Portfolios of the Poor*, 88.

[77] Collins, *Portfolios of the Poor*, 110–111.

The Smart Savings Card from the Opportunity International

Along with mobile banking units in the form of armed and secure vehicles that drive directly to clients, the Opportunity International Bank of Malawi (OIBM) is taking advantage of technology in order to help poor people save money. OIBM began issuing "smart cards" with the client's biometric identification embedded on a chip. This has allowed clients to access their accounts through ATMs in convenient locations where they live and has significantly reduced the time it takes to complete transactions at the bank. This helps keep costs down for both the institution and the client.[78] The Malawian practice of greedy relatives seizing the assets of a widow makes these cards extremely valuable for women who find themselves in this unfortunate position, as only they will be able to use the card.[79]

Offering clients a place to put their savings can be cumbersome and costly. In many countries, government regulation requires microfinance institutions to go through an often-painful process of becoming a formal bank in order to accept client deposits. In addition, they may not have the full support of the donors that provide financial support. According to the Consultative Group to Assist the Poor (CGAP), a consortium of 33 public and private developing agencies that have come together to develop large-scale permanent financial services for the poor, "some donors think of microfinance exclusively as a support for enterprises, not as a multipurpose household financial management tool. Many believe that savings-based

---

[78] Opportunity International, "Technology," http://opportunity.org/what-we-do/products-and-services/global-technology#.UXivCLXqmkI (accessed 2 January 2014).
[79] Malawi Human Rights Commission, "Cultural Practices and their Impact on the Enjoyment of Human Rights, Particularly the Rights of Women and Children in Malawi," Publication date unknown (found at http://www.med col.mw/commhealth/publications/cultural_practices_report.pdf (accessed 5 January 2014), 23.

groups cannot mobilize loans that are large enough to create or develop microenterprises."[80]

As the CGAP comment suggests, the microfinance industry is ripe for a paradigm shift away from loan-centric programs to ones offering additional services, but this needs to happen at all levels, including donors, investors, microfinance institutions, and even clients. Most donor cash earmarked for microfinance is coming from industrial economies like the United States. The dream of starting with nothing and creating wealth is what typically attracts donors—which accounts for why microfinance institutions print color brochures displaying success stories that tout women who borrowed money and used it to develop thriving businesses. Accounts of people who receive long-term job training and who slowly save up to create a better life for their families fail to stir the passions of many donors whose persistent thirst for rags to riches stories causes these other examples often to be left out of the brochure.

What the poor need and have been asking for in addition to loans are savings, insurance, and job training—and some microfinance institutions have been listening to this call for structural changes.[81] One organization, the Bank Rakyat Indonesia (BRI), has tapped into the power of savings and become one of the most successful microfinance institutions in the developing world. In 1998, in response to a financial crisis in Indonesia, BRI reorganized into three divisions: Corporate Banking, Retail Banking, and Microbanking.[82] Realizing that many of the poor put disposable income into lotteries, they

---

[80] Jessica Matthews and Richard Rosenberg, *Community-Managed Loan Funds: Which Ones Work?*, CGAP Focus Note, No. 36 (Washington, DC: The World Bank, May 2006), 7. Note: The authors point out that this statement is an assertion and not completely supported.

[81] "I can't tell you how many times I've heard women clients in our network ask, 'Why can't I save for my child's education, instead of taking out another loan to pay for it?'" Quote from an interview with Mary Ellen Iskenderian, CEO of Women's World Banking. See: Jeremy Caplan, "Microfinance Still Hums, Despite Global Financial Crisis," *Time*, 3 December 2008, http://www.time.com/time/business/article/0,8599,1863443,00.html (accessed 2 January 2014).

[82] Hans Dieter Seibel, "The Microbanking Division of Bank Rakyat Indonesia: A Flagship of Micro-finance in Asia," in *Small Customers, Big Market: Commercial Banks in Micro-Finance*, ed. by Malcolm Harper and Sukhwinder Arora (Rugby, UK: Practical Action, 2005), 4–5.

created a voluntary savings program in the Microbanking Division with a lottery component. This essentially worked by setting the gross interest rate at 13%, with savers receiving 11.5%, while BRI put 1.5% into a lottery fund. Periodically, BRI would hold a drawing and one of the savers would receive the balance of the lottery fund. This proved to be their most attractive savings product; and by June 2003, BRI's customer savings accounts swelled to nearly thirty million (about 50% of the households in Indonesia), with an astonishing borrower-to-saver ratio of roughly 1:10 (i.e. for every one person that takes a loan, ten people have savings accounts without taking a loan).[83] BRI's success provides further evidence that given the right protection and incentives, poor people will and do become savers.

In addition to savings, livelihood training is another area that some microfinance institutions have focused on with increasing success. BASIX, a microfinance institution operating in southern India, includes livelihood promotion services as a key element in its microfinance program. In a recent social rating survey, Micro-Credit Ratings International (M-CRIL) reports that BASIX clients are offered "a range of agricultural services including soil testing, advice on improved seed and agricultural practices and provision of market linkages (selected crops—cotton, potatoes) or veterinary support services for dairy."[84] This type of training makes sense given that most of its clients are agricultural workers (39% of them do not own land)[85] who do not have the wherewithal to launch entrepreneurial ventures. BASIX is also working towards promoting organic agricultural practices, which poor agricultural workers sorely need considering the ever-increasing costs of fertilizers and pesticides.[86]

The first chapter of this book laid out an argument to direct giving toward programs aimed at helping the poor flourish through their own efforts. This chapter has introduced microfinance as a highly effective method to direct financial resources to programs that do just that. After tracing microfinance's historical roots, this chapter has also made the case for organizations to offer a wide variety of

---

[83] Seibel, "Microbanking," 6.

[84] Micro-Credit Ratings International, "BASIX Social Rating 2007," http://www.m-cril.com/pdf/Rating-Reports/BASIX-Social-Rating-2007-M-CRIL.pdf, 9 (accessed 1 January 2014).

[85] Micro-Credit Ratings International, "BASIX Social Rating 2007," 14.

[86] Micro-Credit Ratings International, "BASIX Social Rating 2007," 15.

financial options to focus on the needs of the poor. The poor need access to savings and insurance just as much, and in some cases more, than they do loans. However, loans still form the core of many programs because mobilizing internal savings is sometimes not enough, particularly for poor entrepreneurs with big dreams. As is the case with businesses in the developed world, outside investors are sometimes needed in order to achieve scale. Nevertheless, it is very important that institutions do not restrict clients from accessing other financial or non-financial services without needing to first take out a loan. The next three chapters will explore issues rooted in faith that need to be addressed in order to chart a healthy path of development finance inspired by faith—a subject covered in the final chapter of the book.

3
Protestant Influences

"Having, First, gained all you can, and, Secondly saved all you can, Then 'give all you can.'"[1]

John Wesley

This chapter will focus on how Protestant forces that dramatically altered the economic and cultural landscape of Europe and the United States prior to the twentieth century have persisted and continue to influence people's notions of wealth and the design and delivery of financial services for the poor throughout the rest of the world today. The first section will revisit the concept of the Protestant Ethic posited by sociologist Max Weber and how it has helped to shape modern America from a philanthropic perspective. The second section will look at how the principle of self-reliance found in the Protestant Ethic relates to the American dream of wealth gained primarily through entrepreneurship. The third section will touch upon the challenge of individualism on group microfinance models. The fourth and final section will present an in-depth case study examining the expansive role members of the Mormon Church have played in microfinance. By looking closely at the intellectual thought and practical work of this particular religious denomination, the chapter will demonstrate how many of the ideas of this uniquely American religion, one that has arguably embraced many principles inherent

---

[1] John Wesley, Sermon 50: "The Use of Money," http://www.umcmission. org/Find-Resources/John-Wesley-Sermons/Sermon-50-The-Use-of-Money (accessed 2 January 2014).

in the Protestant Ethic to a high degree, illuminate a myriad of economic issues rooted in those ideals. This is particularly relevant for the design and delivery of microfinance models in developing countries, where these influences can have a subtle, but powerful effect on communities.

The Protestant Ethic revisited

In his seminal essay *The Protestant Ethic and the Spirit of Capitalism*, sociologist Max Weber states his objective as clarifying "the part which religious forces have played in forming the developing web of our specifically worldly modern culture."[2] He poses the question of how religious beliefs and the practice of religion provide psychological sanctions that not only give direction to practical conduct, but also hold individuals to that conduct.[3] Moreover, he asks what aspects of capitalistic culture we can trace back to religious forces.[4] Written in 1904, Weber's work has proven both influential and controversial as some believe it illuminates genuine bilateral connections between religion and capitalism, while others have sought to discredit it as merely a treatise of sweeping generalizations. One could argue that the persistence of this debate through the present day lends some credence to some of the connections Weber proposed.

Weber's central argument rests upon the premise that Puritanism stripped down not only religious practices, but also people themselves. According to Weber, Puritanism nurtured pessimistic individualism,[5] expressed in English Puritan literature as a distrust of friendships and reliance on God as one's sole confidant.[6] He buttresses his argument by contrasting Bunyan's *Pilgrim's Progress* as a tribute to the faithful Puritan who thinks only of his own salvation with Machiavelli's remarks on Catholic Florentines putting their "native city higher than the fear for the salvation of their souls."[7] He also asks how a religious group so superior in social organization can be connected

---

[2] Max Weber, *The Protestant Ethic and the Spirit of Capitalism* (Mineola, NY: Dover Publications, 2003), 90.
[3] Weber, *Protestant Ethic*, 97.
[4] Weber, *Protestant Ethic*, 91.
[5] Weber, *Protestant Ethic*, 105.
[6] Weber, *Protestant Ethic*, 106.
[7] Weber, *Protestant Ethic*, 107.

with the tendency to tear individuals away from the close ties that bind them to this world.[8]

For the Puritans, wasting time was the deadliest of sins because idleness gives way to temptation and distracts a person from the pursuit of a righteous life.[9] Ultimately, Weber connects the Protestant Ethic with the spirit of capitalism by equating the Protestant use of the *call* as "God's commandment of the individual to work for the divine glory" with Adam Smith's promotion of the specialization of occupations. A man without a calling lacked the systematic, methodical character demanded by worldly asceticism.[10] According to the Puritans, if the elect labored in his calling, God would show him ways to profit—and he must take advantage of these opportunities.[11] Furthermore, pursuit of wealth was only negative if it led to idleness.[12]

After some controversial remarks on the Puritans believing they had effectively replaced Jews as the chosen ones, Weber sketches some of the stark details of their asceticism. Reminiscent of ancient Sparta, sports were accepted only for the rational purpose of physical efficiency and many of the arts were viewed as a waste of time. He attributes the powerful tendency toward uniformity of life, which helped to standardize capitalistic production, to the Puritan repudiation of all idolatry of the flesh. While the spirit of capitalism existed prior to the Reformation, Weber argues that the ethos of ascetic Protestantism wielded a heavy influence on capitalistic culture and production.[13] Throughout the essay Weber alludes to a bilateral relationship between the capitalistic ethos and ascetic Protestantism, where their efficiency and austerity easily feed off one another.

Weber begins the section on capitalism by quoting from a letter written by a father to his son, which he describes as the spirit of capitalism in its purest form and which he later uses to tie into Protestant asceticism. Railing against idleness and equating both time and credit with money, the father admonishes further, "After industry and frugality, nothing contributes more to the raising of a young man in the world than punctuality and justice in all his dealings: therefore

---

[8] Weber, *Protestant Ethic*, 108.
[9] Weber, *Protestant Ethic*, 157.
[10] Weber, *Protestant Ethic*, 161.
[11] Weber, *Protestant Ethic*, 162.
[12] Weber, *Protestant Ethic*, 163.
[13] Weber, *Protestant Ethic*, 166–70.

never keep borrowed money an hour beyond the time you promised, lest a disappointment shut up your friend's purse forever."[14] What is surprising is that these words come not from a strict Calvinist, but from none other than Benjamin Franklin, an ardent proponent of Protestant ethical ideals despite himself being a religious skeptic.

The historical example of Franklin helped to tie the Protestant Ethic to American ideals. Another figure emerges in American history, who was a contemporary of Weber and in many ways came to symbolize much of Weber's work in this area: John D. Rockefeller. In the words of biographer Ron Chernow, "John D. Rockefeller was the Protestant work ethic in its purest form, leading a life so consistent with Weber's classical essay that it reads like his spiritual biography."[15] Rockefeller's name has become synonymous with wealth accumulation, and his history as both as a nineteenth-century robber baron and twentieth-century philanthropist reveals the duality of the Protestant Ethic expressed in America. It is doubtful that Weber personally knew Rockefeller, but a closer look at his life illuminates some of the concepts and issues discussed throughout this chapter.

His own father, a drifter and charlatan, often left the family for several months at a time, leaving John D. Rockefeller and his five siblings under the spiritual guidance of their puritanical mother. A serious child and sober Baptist, young Rockefeller began his career in 1845 at the age of sixteen as a bookkeeper in Cleveland, Ohio. Chernow points out that Rockefeller was shaped by both a nationwide economic depression during his adolescence and his strict Baptist upbringing. The economic downturn fueled an evangelical religious resurgence that led to the Businessman's Revival in 1857, a group of businessmen who believed that it was a divine punishment for sins of extravagance and who met during their lunch hour to pray and swear off indulgences;[16] as Rockefeller would later recall of his early days in business, "What a school—the school of adversity and stress—to train a boy in!"[17] Indeed, it is difficult not to see the connection between Rockefeller's life and Weber's description of

---

[14] Weber, *Protestant Ethic*, 49.
[15] Ron Chernow, *Titan: The Life of John D. Rockefeller, Sr.* (New York: Vintage Books, 1998), 55.
[16] Chernow, *Rockefeller*, 57.
[17] Chernow, *Rockefeller*, 57.

modern capitalists influenced by ascetic Protestantism: "they were men who had grown up in the hard school of life, calculating and daring at the same time, above all temperate and reliable, shrewd and completely devoted to their business, with strict bourgeois opinions and principles."[18]

By 1870 at the age of thirty one Rockefeller had established the Standard Oil Company. Within ten years Standard Oil controlled over ninety percent of the world's oil industry, making Rockefeller a multimillionaire. Rockefeller applied a rather misshapen view of the Protestant self-reliance ideal to Standard Oil, which had far-reaching ramifications. He perceived it as a single entity when in fact it was comprised of several oil refineries that he had quickly acquired controlling interests in through various tactics that garnered him much hatred in his time—primarily through secret deals for lower transportation costs with the railroads that allowed Standard Oil to undercut the prices of its competitors. In an industry that grew extremely quickly due to a sudden increase in demand for oil, Rockefeller saw this as an opportunity to protect the entire industry from collapse in a volatile market filled with reckless refiners operating in an unregulated economy. A shrewd businessman, he pressured and cajoled other refiners to join Standard Oil. Those that spurned his proposals often found themselves out of business when they could not compete in a price war. This was true of one of his church friends who refused to join Standard Oil and found himself bankrupt and losing his life's savings. So embittered was the man by this episode, that he never set foot in a church again.[19] By consolidating and streamlining the entire industry under his leadership, he saw himself as a savior, and was often stunned by the criticism hurled at him by the general public. In the upcoming case study in this chapter on the Mormons we will see some similarities between that group and Rockefeller's application of self-reliance both to himself and to the unified entity that he controlled.

A true adherent to the principles of the Protestant Ethic, Rockefeller worked extremely hard for the first half of his life and then retired from business to devote the remainder of his life directing a significant portion of his immense wealth to worthy causes. In

---

[18] Weber, *Protestant Ethic*, 69.
[19] Chernow, *Rockefeller*, 147.

developing a systematic method of charity based on business principles of accountability through the conditional grant, he revolutionized modern philanthropy by ensuring that his wealth targeted projects and institutions in a way that promised maximum efficiency and effectiveness. One of the largest grant-making institutions in the world, the Rockefeller Foundation still continues to provide over a hundred million dollars a year towards social, economic, health, and environmental initiatives.

Rockefeller's philosophy of hard work, self-reliance, and thrift was not lost on his immediate family, where his five children were subjected to his stringent pecuniary ways. He and his wife Cettie did their best to shield their children from the outside world, educating them at home and instilling in them strict religious values. He doled out very meager allowances and concealed his wealth from them to such an extent that even as young adults they had little idea of the magnitude of his fortune.[20] During high school, his only son Junior (as he was called) endured long walks to school each morning while watching much less wealthy classmates drive past in expensive carriages.[21] The children could never quite escape the long shadow of their father and Junior especially struggled from physical and emotional breakdowns throughout his adolescence and young adulthood. While the strict values upbringing may have taken a toll on the younger Rockefeller, he eventually hit his professional stride and found his calling after shifting from a Standard Oil executive role to overseeing the Rockefeller Foundation. The Foundation flourished under his leadership and expanded its support of the arts and a variety of social causes, including medical research. Remaining true to the religious beliefs ingrained in him since childhood, throughout his life Junior personally gave vast sums to Protestant ecumenical institutions such as Union Theological Seminary and the World Council of Churches.

Self-reliance and the limits of the American dream

Weber's often cited claim that most people are now stuck in an "iron cage" of capitalism while the spirit of religious asceticism has long

---

[20] Chernow, *Rockefeller*, 232.
[21] Chernow, *Rockefeller*, 232.

escaped the cage deftly captures the ethos of modern America.[22] Despite persistent cycles of religious revivals, particularly among Protestant evangelical sects, America has essentially left behind its puritanical past and fully embraced ostentatious living and a vacuous popular culture—with the rare exception of the Mormons, who will be discussed in the next section. Nonetheless, the promise of economic and social mobility through entrepreneurship in a healthy and competitive marketplace remains a steadfast fixture in American life. The American dream, grounded in rugged individualism and self-reliance, continues to draw many immigrants to her shores, fueling innovation, and nurturing the prospect of eudemonia for those wishing to take risks and exercise creativity. But self-reliance taken to the extreme can warp into self-centeredness and rejection of interdependence, ultimately leading to alienation and anti-social behavior. This common misinterpretation loses the point Ralph Waldo Emerson, the American essayist, lecturer, and poet, tried to make in his essay on the topic where he argued for self-reliance as striving for freethinking and non-conformity in a world where others presume to know your path better than you do.[23]

Self-reliance runs deep in America with its myriad expressions from gritty salt of the earth personalities to disciples of Ayn Rand's Objectivist philosophy. Her view of selfishness as a virtue has influenced powerful people in America such as former Federal Reserve Chairman Alan Greenspan, who for many years held several of the levers to the American financial system.[24] These distortions of self-reliance have also found a subtle expression in American culture through movies depicting the archetypal rugged male lead played by actors such as John Wayne and Bruce Willis that spurn help from others as they take on the role of maverick saviors with bravado. As America stumbles down a twisting path of its own *Pilgrim's Progress*, these cultural messages have only served to disconnect people as they seek out personal power without the requisite interdependence necessary for human fulfillment and happiness. While America still

---

[22] Weber, *Protestant Ethic*, 181.

[23] Ralph Waldo Emerson, *Self Reliance and Other Essays* (New York: Dover, 1993), 23.

[24] Common Dreams, "Alan Shrugged: Greenspan, Ayn Rand and Their God That Failed," https://www.commondreams.org/view/2008/10/25-6 (accessed 2 January 2014).

struggles with this legacy, anybody who thinks the Protestant Ethic is dead in Europe need only consider Germany's recent fervor in exerting pressure on her southern European Union neighbors to enact and maintain economic austerity measures.

This phenomenon of personal and cultural disconnection is elegantly captured in Robert Putnam's book, *Bowling Alone: The Collapse and Revival of American Community*. Here Putnam sketches out the erosion of civic engagement and close relationships between neighbors in America that has led to a quick disintegration of social capital. The usual social culprits he points to are increased divorce rates, suburban sprawl, and women entering the workforce. All of these contributions are up for debate, but it is the main indictment of television's role in occupying people's time (which used to be spent doing things like bowling and going to church) and contributing to the disintegration of social capital that drives home the reality that Americans are becoming more and more alienated from their fellow human beings. Here we see in the steady decline an ultimate betrayal of the human spirit in wasting one's life through idleness as a result of alienation from fellow human beings—the fulfillment of the Puritan's worst fears and an inevitability of rejecting interdependence by erroneously confusing it with dependence.

American self-reliance has also found a new expression through entrepreneurship. The term "entrepreneurship," once reserved for those who started companies, now encompasses a wider spectrum of usage. Successful and self-determined entrepreneurs like Reid Hoffman (founder of LinkedIn) are encouraging employees to be more entrepreneurial in both their personal lives and in the workplace.[25] In fact, he wrote an entire book on the topic entitled the "Startup of You."[26] Admittedly, the root word with its European origin subtly evokes the American dream and all that it represents with elegant imagery. But while entrepreneurial qualities might be valued in society and many organizations, the adoption and increasingly excessive use of this buzzword can lead to confusion as it encroaches on the territory of other more descriptive words. Employees might be

---

[25] Reid Hoffman and Ben Casnocha, *The Start-up of You: Adapt to the Future, Invest in Yourself, and Transform Your Career* (New York: Crown Business, 2012), 23.
[26] Hoffman and Casnocha, *Startup of You*.

asked to show more entrepreneurism in instances where more suitable words such as "creativity" or "initiative" ought to be used. As we shall soon see, this word carries profound and perhaps problematic implications in the field of microfinance.

Howard Stevenson of Harvard Business School defines entrepreneurship as "a process by which individuals—either on their own or inside organizations—pursue opportunities without regard to the resources they currently control."[27] Given this definition, the main difference between "standard" employees and entrepreneurs is that the former are resource-oriented, while the latter are opportunity-oriented. Furthermore, entrepreneurs succeed by pursuing opportunities that possess varying levels of risk. Ultimately, entrepreneurship is best suited for those who are comfortable taking on additional risk—and the best entrepreneurs often see downside risk in *not* accepting a challenging opportunity.

Incidentally, despite its reputation and history of strong support for start-ups, this is not the main engine that drives America's economy. In fact, a 2012 report put out by the Organization for Economic Cooperation and Development ranked America second to last (with Canada ranked last) in percentage of start-ups. Mexico was ranked first, followed by Slovenia—two countries with much smaller economies than Canada and the United States.[28] While the number of start-ups in America did increase during the Great Recession (2007–2009), that figure quickly dropped as the American economy gained strength. It is clear that Americans turn to entrepreneurship in times of need.

Against this backdrop of the Protestant Ethic and modern social trends, the strong American influence on the design and delivery of microfinance programs aimed at poverty alleviation requires further examination, particularly given the potential exportation and promotion of self-reliance under the label of entrepreneurship. A majority of microfinance clients are entrepreneurs. This is partially

---

[27] Howard H. Stevenson, "A Paradigm of Entrepreneurship," in *Strategic Management Journal*, Vol. 11, Special Issue: Corporate Entrepreneurship (Hoboken, NJ: John Wiley, Summer 1990), 23.

[28] Jordan Weissmann, "Think We're the Most Entrepreneurial Country In the World? Not So Fast," *The Atlantic*, 2 October 2012, http://www.theatlantic.com/business/archive/2012/10/think-were-the-most-entrepreneurial-country-in-the-world-not-so-fast/26310J2/ (accessed 2 January 2014).

due to the legacy of microcredit and its focus on small business loans that continues to form the backbone of most microfinance institutions' programs. Micro-entrepreneurs who take on debt to create and grow businesses also help microfinance institutions grow as they pay back loans with interest. While this system provides benefits to a small segment of the population, it also leaves a larger one behind. The following quote from Muhammad Yunus of the Grameen Bank offers a worldview representative of most microfinance institutions that presents a legitimate challenge to the goal of helping the world's poor through microfinance:

> If all of us started to view every single human being, even the barefooted one begging in the street, as a potential entrepreneur, then we could build an economic system that would allow each man or woman to explore his or her economic potential.[29]

While this statement may illicit a positive emotional response from westerners, particularly Americans who place a high value on entrepreneurship, what Yunus fails to point out is that just like Americans during the Great Recession many of the world's poor become entrepreneurs out of necessity and not necessarily choice. In the latter case this has become institutionalized over time. It is not clear how much Yunus was influenced by American Protestant ideals during the time he spent studying at Vanderbilt in Nashville, but his sentiments certainly resonate with the Protestant Ethic ideal of self-reliance as it has now become synonymous with entrepreneurship.

International economic development academics and practitioners are beginning to attack the entrepreneurship-centric microfinance model as short-sighted and misaligned with the true needs of the world's poor. After studying the economic lives of the poor by personally interviewing them around the world, the authors of *Poor Economics* make a poignant observation about entrepreneurship: "There are more than a billion people who run their own farm or business, but most of them do this because they have no other options."[30] As the authors point out, in many poor societies, the most

---

[29] Muhammad Yunus, *Banker to the Poor* (New York: Public Affairs, 2003), 207.
[30] Abhijit V. Banerjee and Esther Duflo, *Poor Economics* (New York: Public Affairs, 2001), 233.

common dream for parents in developing countries is for their children to secure economic stability through obtaining a government job.[31] For people in these countries, starting a business is merely the default career when their own access to social and economic mobility remains restricted. In any society, there are people whose calling may indeed be starting a business or even taking over one started by others. Giving them access to credit can have a dramatic and positive effect on their business, their lives, and their community at large by institutionalizing and legitimizing entrepreneurship.

But giving poor people credit can have damaging effects if organizations employ misguided approaches such as pushing their clients to become entrepreneurs whether they are suited to this role or not. Despite increased awareness among economic development experts, microfinance institutions, principally backed by American funding, continue to offer only business loans to the communities where they serve. At its worst, this model smacks of colonialism. In the book *Portfolios of the Poor* (first mentioned in Chapter 3) the authors make this connection clear, "One element of inflexibility in microfinance is the insistence by some lenders that all loans be invested in businesses."[32] This is further exacerbated by colorful brochures and other marketing materials that employ rags-to-riches stories that appeal to western donors and investors.

Given differing attitudes in terms of risk aversion, characterizing everyone as a potential entrepreneur places some people at a distinct disadvantage. Taking out loans for business ventures is not for everyone, and what amounts to a small risk to some might represent a perilous undertaking to others. Additionally, entrepreneurship often requires small business owners to compete for customers—an activity that challenges some people's very nature. Strictly speaking, human beings have the *potential* to be entrepreneurs, but not every personality is suited to that type of activity.[33] Again, entrepreneurship in its

---

[31] Banerjee and Duflo, *Poor Economics*, 227.

[32] Daryl Collins, Jonathon Morduch, Stuart Rutherford, and Orlanda Ruthven, *Portfolios of the Poor* (Princeton, NJ: Princeton University Press, 2009), 63.

[33] Hurst and Lusardi estimate the percentage of entrepreneurs in the United States at only 13%. Developing countries, however, most likely retain a higher percentage of entrepreneurs (See: Erik Hurst and Annamaria Lusardi, "Do Household Savings Encourage Entrepreneurship?" in *Overcoming Barriers to Entrepreneurship in the United States*, ed. Diana Furchgott-Roth (Lanham, MD: Lexington Books, 2008), 50).

strictest sense is a suitable vocation for some people who believe that this is their calling—and supporting them is a good thing as it may lead to job creation within communities. However, microfinance institutions that try to turn all of their clients into business owners may indeed help some of them, but this also sets others up for failure. As Chapter 2 illuminated, the poor need a paradigm that addresses their fundamental needs with a healthy suite of financial services rather than one that seeks to turn everyone into a small business owner.

In order to be effective in alleviating poverty, organizations will need to offer additional products like savings and insurance to capture those needs and put people on a long-term path of financial independence. This is not an easy task, particularly in trying to cultivate a culture of savings in geographies where historically food grew in abundance year round and communities shared those resources instead of needing to save up stores of food to last through a cold winter. In such societies, particularly in the global South, norms around social capital also dictate that resources belong to the community and one is obligated to share extras with neighbors and family rather than putting them away as personal savings. Nevertheless, by targeting the *true* entrepreneurs (i.e. those that choose this profession out of a passion for it) and putting additional focus on those individuals through training and other technical assistance, the businesses they create might then be in a better position to employ others who excel in creativity and innovation, or who are just motivated by a desire to work. In an article calling for increased funding towards primary and secondary education in developing countries, journalist Nicolas Kristof effectively captures a healthy perspective that also applies to how microfinance promoters should be viewing the problem and how to formulate solutions:"Talent is universal … opportunity is not."[34]

Individualism vs. the power of groups and social connections

The implications of the subtle, but powerful effect of Protestant asceticism are pervasive throughout microfinance and extend

---

[34] Nicolas Kristof, "From South Sudan to Yale," *The New York Times,* 28 March 2012, http://www.nytimes.com/2012/03/29/opinion/kristof-from-south-sudan-to-yale.html?_r=0 (accessed 2 January 2014).

beyond entrepreneurship to aspects such as the group models that were so effective in their early history. Much the same as the person has been stripped down and seduced into a hyper-efficiency mindset, so have models used to provide financial access for the poor. Instead of a shift towards robust credit union cooperatives that offer a wide range of personal and professional services within a solidarity group structure aimed at truly helping each other, we now have a tilting preference towards bare-bones individual credit models. This shift in microfinance has sprung primarily from ever-increasing commercial bank and profit-seeking investor involvement, heavily influenced by western banking sustained through the centuries by an ascetic undercurrent.

Microfinance expert and sometimes gadfly to the industry, Malcolm Harper, makes a compelling argument that microfinance providers should actually be moving away from group models, since the regular group meetings are burdensome to the clients who repeatedly ask for individual loans.[35] He claims that these labor-intensive systems ultimately benefit the microfinance institutions and commercial banks that run them because they are less expensive to operate (collections can be made all at once), group liability reduces delinquencies (less risky for the lender), and members become trapped in perpetual cycles of debt when a loan is required in order to remain active in the group (which increases profits for the lender).[36] Furthermore, he downplays the need for group meetings as a regrettable short-term necessity to which those in the developed world are not subjected: "We do not have to attend meetings to obtain financial services."[37] He concludes that the continued focus on group delivery methods harkens back to the biblical belief that the poor will always be with us.[38] For him, what is wrong with microfinance is the assumption that it will never really work as a cure, but only to alleviate poverty. The view that the poor can never be like "us" means that instead of looking for ways to eradicate poverty and "to put ourselves out of business" the development industry operates

---

[35] Malcolm Harper, "What's wrong with groups," in *What's Wrong with Microfinance*, ed. Thomas Dichter and Malcolm Harper (Warwickshire, UK: Practical Action Publishing, 1997), 44.

[36] Harper, "What's wrong with groups," 43.

[37] Harper, "What's wrong with groups," 43.

[38] Mark 14:7(Revised Standard Version).

as though it will never go away.[39] This sentiment has been shared by Muhammad Yunus with his often quoted claim that one day there should be poverty museums.

Harper makes persuasive arguments when seen through the lens of a culture embedded in strong remnants of Protestant asceticism. However, in glossing over the positive aspects of group membership, he underestimates the power of these groups to transform people's lives, particularly for women. Group meetings are not simply venues to disburse and collect money, but a venue where members share ideas, both business and personal. Many organizations schedule family and community empowerment programs during these meetings to tackle and discuss issues such as sexual health, proper sanitation methods, nutrition, and prevention of domestic violence. For some, these few hours a month, rather than being a burden, take on a central importance in their lives, particularly in societies that place an extremely high value on social connection. Perhaps the question should not be whether the poor should be like us, but rather whether we in the western world should instead be learning from the high value they place on family and community.

In fact, understanding the significance of social connections in other societies remains a major stumbling block for many westerners, which according to sociologist Richard Nisbett has its roots in Greek thought. According to Nisbett, the Greek ideal of personal agency, connected to individualism, contrasts sharply with its Chinese counterpart of harmony.[40] While Greek Aristotelian logic encouraged linear logic within a static world, the Confucian stance toward life proposed that the "world is constantly changing and is full of contradictions."[41] Instead of breaking things and people down into individual objects that have free agency, Chinese thought aims towards interdependent social harmony—something seen up through the present day.[42] These differences appear in architecture, where in the West the aim is to create something unique that stands out from the others, whereas in China a *feng shui* expert works alongside the

---

[39] Harper, "What's wrong with groups," 47.
[40] Richard E. Nisbett, *Geography of Thought: How Asians and Westerners Think Differently ... and Why* (New York: Free Press, 2003), 5.
[41] Nisbett, *Geography of Thought,* 13.
[42] Nisbett, *Geography of Thought,* 19.

architect to ensure that the new building can be unique, but must maintain a sense of harmony with its surroundings.[43]

Context is so important in East Asia that Protestant Ethic ideals such as self-reliance and individualism as expressed by Western businesspeople in particular often lead to misunderstandings. For example, the case of a Japanese-Australian sugar contract during the 1970s underscores the differences between independent and interdependent societies. Australian sugar producers contracted with Japanese refiners to deliver sugar for a fixed price over a five-year period. When the price on the world market dropped dramatically, the Japanese argued that the contract needed to be renegotiated on the basis that the context had drastically changed. The Australians, however, refused to make any changes because of the circumstances, which they saw as independent of the original contract.[44]

Nisbett shares the following story to illustrate what he calls as "The Idea moves west," whereby values of individuality, freedom, rationality, and universalism grew more dominant as civilization moved westward from ancient Babylon to the United States:

> I once knew a very distinguished and well-placed social scientist, a crusty Scottish-American Presbyterian steeped in Calvinist rectitude. He had a son who was also a social scientist and who had to struggler from time to time to sustain his career during the 1970s, when jobs were scarce in the U.S. My colleague would sometimes state proudly that, although it would have been easy for him to do so, he had never intervened to help his son's situation. The colleague's Anglo-Saxon Protestant friends would nod their approval of the justice in this stance in the face of the personal pain they knew the colleague had experienced. His Jewish and Catholic colleagues, with their more Continental values, would stare in shocked disbelief at his lack of family feeling. At a level slightly more scientific than this anecdote: We generally find that it is the white Protestants among American participants in our studies who show the most "Western" patterns of behavior and that Catholics and minority group members, including African Americans and Hispanics, are shifted somewhat toward Eastern patterns.[45]

---

[43] Nisbett, *Geography of Thought,* 23.
[44] Nisbett, *Geography of Thought,* 66.
[45] Nisbett, *Geography of Thought,* 70.

While generalizations regarding the Protestant Ethic and who might ascribe to it carry the potential for scrutiny, if one's objective is to understand inspiration and influences, further reflection is helpful. The next section will attempt to draw out some of these inspirations and influences through looking closely at Mormon engagement in microfinance.

Case study: Mormon engagement in microfinance

The Church of Jesus Christ of Latter-day Saints traces its history to 1830 when a young man named Joseph Smith, Jr. from Palmyra, New York published the *Book of Mormon*. Considered the most sacred text in the Mormon religion, the *Book of Mormon* recounts the words of various prophets who purportedly lived on the North American continent during the two millennia preceding Christ and several hundred years after his death. Smith claims to have discovered these words written on several gold plates that he found in a cave in Palmyra after an angel named Moroni appeared to him in a vision and revealed the location of the plates. Following a move westward to Ohio, Smith stated that his ultimate goal, as recounted through one of his revelations in 1831, was to re-establish a New Jerusalem in the United Sates: "Independence, Missouri, is the place for the City of Zion and the temple."[46] After several moves westward with his growing congregation of followers, including a brief stay in Missouri,[47] Smith eventually settled in Nauvoo, Illinois,[48] becoming its mayor and also running for the President of the United States in the 1844 election. He was killed that same year by an angry mob shortly after his arrest for giving the order to destroy the town's sole printing press when it began publishing articles criticizing Mormon doctrine and practices.

---

[46] The Church of Jesus Christ of Latter-day Saints, *The Doctrine and Covenants of the Church of Jesus Christ of Latter-Day Saints, The Pearl of Great Price* (Salt Lake City, UT: Church of Jesus Christ of Latter-Day Saints, 2013), 57:1.

[47] Mormons indeed settled the area in and around Independence, Missouri in 1831. However, tensions between Mormons and non-Mormons rose to such a high degree that in 1838 war broke out between Mormons and the Missouri State Militia and following that war all Mormons were expelled by the governor under Missouri Executive Order 44.

[48] The original name of the town was Commerce, and was changed to Nauvoo after the Mormons purchased it in 1840.

In 1846, Smith's successor, Brigham Young, led a mass exodus of roughly 70,000 Mormons westward into the Salt Lake Valley in what is now the state of Utah. Many parts of Utah are covered in desert landscapes, and Mormons have drawn several parallels between their own path and that of the Israelite's journey out of Egypt to the Promised Land. The struggle for survival amidst a barren and inhospitable wilderness reinforced the need for a tight intra-dependency within the greater Mormon "family," a unifier whose image endures through the present day both culturally and theologically. Through hard work, perseverance, and collective effort the Mormon settlers eventually flourished in the Salt Lake Valley and the surrounding area. Beginning in 1849, Mormon leaders actively lobbied the US congress for statehood, eventually winning that right by the end of the nineteenth century. With its headquarters in Salt Lake City, Utah, today the Mormon Church claims a total worldwide membership of over fourteen million members, with two million of those in the state of Utah.[49]

While the Mormon Church does admire and recognize the works of the Protestant reformers, it was technically not founded on principles of the Reformation and is generally not considered a "true" Protestant denomination.[50] Nevertheless, as a non-Catholic Christian religion developed within the United States in the mid-nineteenth century, contemporary Mormonism certainly retains many cultural aspects of what others would deem ascetical, or even Protestant, in nature. For example, Mormon Scripture sets a clear tone that its adherents need to maintain a strong work ethic. So strong, in fact, that their scriptures frame it as commandment: "Thou shalt not be idle; for he that is idle shall not eat the bread nor wear the garments of the laborer."[51] Restricting the use of tobacco, alcohol, and many caffeinated beverages,[52] along with the admonishment to

---

[49] Mormon Newsroom, "Facts and Statistics," http://www.mormonnews room.org/facts-and-stats (accessed 2 January 2014).

[50] Jan Shipps writes: "Despite a value structure and belief in Jesus Christ which Mormons share with middle-class American Protestants, the Saints have not been absorbed into Protestantism." See: Jan Shipps, "The Prophet Puzzle: Suggestions Leading Toward a More Comprehensive Interpretation of Joseph Smith" *The Prophet Puzzle* (Salt Lake City: Signature Books, 1997), 27–28.

[51] Church of Jesus Christ of Latter-day Saints, *The Doctrine and Covenants*, 42:42.

[52] Church of Jesus Christ of Latter-day Saints, *The Doctrine and Covenants*, 89:5–8.

wear plain garments, is further evidence of ascetical insistence in the Scriptures.[53] It would be a mistake to simply hang the label of Puritanical asceticism around the necks of the Latter-day Saints. But the heavy emphasis on self-reliance and work ethic strongly links Mormon culture with that of Weber's idealized capitalistic society.

Mormon scholars are actively engaged in an internal debate over the values of work and how they relate to Mormon culture. In his response to Douglas Davies' book, *The Mormon Culture of Salvation: Force, Grace and Glory*, former professor of philosophy at Brigham Young University (BYU), David Paulson, underscores activity as a key Mormon value—with work, particularly temple work, as a form of worship.[54] In his analysis, Paulson believes that Davies does not go far enough in equating work itself with the work of God, grounding his argument in the words both from Christ in the Gospel of John[55] and from the Hebrew word *avodah*, which means worship but is derived from the word for labor and service.[56]

Similarly, Professor Hugh Nibley of BYU attempts to address what appear to be cultural parallels to Weber's caution against the rational acquisition of wealth (that often results in an accumulation of capital through the ascetic compulsion to save).[57] He admonishes church members to rethink their relationship to work, wealth, and the duty of helping others, by first reinterpreting Mormon notions of idleness:

> An idler in the Lord's book is one who is not working for the building up of the kingdom of God on earth and the establishment of Zion, no matter how hard he may be working to satisfy his own greed. Latter-day Saints prefer to ignore that distinction as they repeat a favorite maxim of their own invention, that the idler shall not eat the bread or wear the clothing of the laborer. And what an ingenious argument they make of it! The director

---

[53] Church of Jesus Christ of Latter-day Saints, *The Doctrine and Covenants*, 42:40.

[54] David L. Paulson and Cory G. Walker, "Work, Worship and Grace," (Salt Lake City: Deseret Books and FARMS Review, 2000), 86.

[55] John 5:17 (Revised Standard Version): "My Father is always at his work to this very day, and I, too, am working."

[56] Paulson and Walker, "Work, Worship and Grace," 87–88.

[57] Weber, *Protestant Ethic*, 171–172.

of a Latter-day Saint Institute was recently astounded when this writer pointed out to him that the ancient teaching that the idler shall not eat the bread of the laborer has always meant that the idle rich shall not eat the bread of the laboring poor, as they always have.[58]

Here we see a prominent Mormon scholar attempting to redirect attention to the Mormon mission of building Zion and its relationship to the poor. He drives his point further:

You are perfectly free to make all the money you can; just as you are perfectly free to break any one of the Ten Commandments, as millions do every day, though God has forbidden it, as he has forbidden seeking for riches. But your behavior once you have entered a covenant with God will be judged by the standards which he sets: "Therefore, if any man shall take of the abundance which I have made and impart not his portion, according to the law of my gospel, unto the poor and the needy, he shall, with the wicked, lift up his eyes in hell, being in torment" (D&C 104:18). A clear reference to the rich man who fed Lazarus the beggar with crumbs in the Gospel of Luke.[59]

Nibley reminds Mormons that building Zion should be the central focus of their efforts, not the pursuit of wealth, which he sees as a common trap Mormons fall into. However, reaching out to the poor and creating a society of equals is a difficult process, the early church leader Brigham Young recognized, that in terms of the wealth distribution would soon be usurped by inequality, for the lion's share going to the most dedicated and competent seekers for it.[60]

As we learn more about Mormon engagement in microfinance in the next section, one central question is how far the church itself should become involved in economic development programs to reach

---

[58] Hugh W. Nibley, *Approaching Zion* (Salt Lake City: Deseret Books and FARMS Review, 1989), 203–251.

[59] Nibley, *Approaching Zion*, 203–251 and Luke 16:23(Revised Standard Version).

[60] Nibley, *Approaching Zion*, 203–251.

out to the poor, particularly on the international stage. As the writers of an in-depth history of Mormon economic development point out:

> With a record of 160 years of persistent effort, few existing organizations have worked longer in the anti-poverty field than the Church of Jesus Christ of Latter-day Saints and probably none has devoted more per-capita effort towards that goal. But the church is a spiritual, not an economic organization; it perceives its charge as the salvation of human souls. In that context, economic well-being, as important as it has been historically, has a lower priority and a lesser claim on the resources of the church.[61]

With its model of sending young missionaries to nearly every country around the world to proselytize and to perform community service, the Mormon Church has indeed attained a vantage point for providing and promoting economic development programs in poverty-stricken communities in developing countries.[62] Given the very strong parallels to the Protestant Ethic and the heavy influence Mormons have on the promotion and spread of microfinance around the world, an exploration of these similarities is necessary.

Microfinance and the Church of Jesus Christ of Latter-day Saints

Early in its history, the Mormon Church learned the sometimes painful consequences of faith groups directly engaging in banking. In 1836, the founder Joseph Smith organized the Kirtland Safety Society Anti-Banking Company, a joint-stock company that provided financial services to church members and others in the surrounding community in Kirtland, Ohio. Within a few years, the bank went broke, and as a result, Smith faced an onslaught of lawsuits. Nevertheless, community members pulled together to compensate the creditors,[63]

---

[61] Garth Mangum and Bruce Blumell, *The Mormons' War on Poverty: A History of LDS Welfare, 1830–1990* (Salt Lake City: University of Utah Press, 1993), 261.

[62] As of April 2013, the Church had 405 active missions with 65,634 full-time missionaries around the world. See President Thomas M. Monson, "Welcome to Conference," *Liahona Magazine*, May 2013, http://www.lds.org/liahona/2013/05/welcome-to-conference (accessed 2 January 2014).

[63] Richard L. Bushman, *Joseph Smith: Rough Stone Rolling* (New York: Vintage Books, 2005), 331.

echoing back to comments that biographer Richard Bushman makes in recounting other financial problems Joseph Smith's family faced early in his life: "all of the debts had to be paid, a point of honor with the Smiths. They would not run out on their creditors as others did."[64] The failure of the Kirtland bank reinforces the challenges faith groups face when they choose to become a source of financial services, reminiscent of the Biblical warning against serving two masters.[65] As a testament to Joseph Smith's powerful charisma, the willingness of community members to cover the bank debt also provides an early glimpse into the Mormon sense of intra-dependency that not only helped in their survival as they moved to Utah, but which has ultimately served them well in business. For Mormons, self-reliance itself is not restricted to individuals, but also extends to family and the entire community of Mormons. Being a Mormon means being part of "one self" in a larger sense; hence showing characteristics of intra-dependence within a single unit, rather than a true interdependence.

Nevertheless, a central tension in this balancing act stems from apparent contradictions in Mormon theology. The Mormon belief in a pre-mortal family that also perpetuates beyond the grave, a family that must learn to stick together through eternity, is compelling in its power to cultivate a sense of intra-dependency.[66] However, this may be confusing to those who not only foster self-reliance, but who are also admonished to have total dependence on God. As Nibley puts it, "if you serve *him* with your whole heart and with your whole soul, you are free from dependence on any other being."[67] While these tensions can certainly be resolved by focusing on establishing a solid relationship with oneself, others and the divine, possible confusion might arise in practical situations when one tries to reconcile those connections. This makes Weber's assessment of the relationship between religion and capitalism a necessary tool to measure how values play out in the marketplace, especially in terms of individualism and asceticism.

Helping others through finance has remained a strong Mormon value since its beginnings. In 2000, Mormon Church members

---

[64] Bushman, *Joseph Smith*, 28.
[65] Luke 16:13 (Revised Standard Version).
[66] The Church of Jesus Christ of Latter-day Saints, "The Family: A Proclamation to the World," http://www.lds.org/library/display/0,4945,161-1-11-1,00.html (accessed 2 January 2014).
[67] Nibley, *Approaching Zion*, 203–251.

Robert Gay, Mike Murray, Joseph Grenny, and Todd Manwaring founded Unitus, a US-based non-profit organization with the goal of fighting global poverty through increasing access to microfinance. Representing the first major foray into microfinance by members of the Mormon Church, Unitus initially provided capital investments and consulting services to financially sustainable microfinance institutions worldwide, grounding its motivation in the Mormon spiritual ideal of creating a united order[68] of Zion on earth:

> Poverty will only be eliminated when a sufficient number of people are filled with this "love of God" that makes us unable to bear anything less than Zion, In short, if we are to succeed we must be motivated not just by a desire to eliminate poverty, but by a commitment to building Zion.[69]

However, some have questioned the way in which Zion is being built through Unitus. As a facilitator for directing commercial funding into the microfinance sector, Unitus assisted large microfinance institutions in becoming more profitable. For example, they helped position SKS Microfinance Limited in India to make an initial public offering (IPO) on 28 July 2010 that in turn raised over USD $350 million and made the firm's founder, Vikram Akula a multimillionaire in the process.[70] In addition to severe criticism surrounding SKS's massive profit generated from working with the poor, that organization was dogged by an investigation into two hundred suicides in the Indian state of Andhra Pradesh in late 2010, only a few months after the IPO. The suicides were attributed to a wave of overindebtedness caused by reckless credit approval standards that allowed for poor people to take on several loans from several different microfinance institutions.

---

[68] Lucas and Woodworth provide an excellent history of the Untied Order. The United Order is the implementation of the divine teachings and commandments encompassed in the law of consecration and stewardship. See James W. Lucas and Warner Woodworth, *Working Toward Zion: Principles of the United Order for the Modern World* (Salt Lake City: Aspen Books, 1996), 17.

[69] Warner Woodworth, Joseph Grenny, and Todd Manwaring, *United for Zion: Principles for Uniting the Saints to Eliminate Poverty* (Orem, UT: Unitus Publications, 2000), 14.

[70] Vikas Bajaj, "Microlender, First in India to Go Public, Trades Higher," *The New York Times*, 16 August 2010, http://www.nytimes.com/2010/08/17/busi ness/global/17micro.html?_r=0 (accessed 3 January 2014).

As the *Wall Street Journal* reported, allegations surfaced that "SKS employees had verbally harassed over-indebted borrowers, forced them to pawn valuable items, incited other borrowers to humiliate them and orchestrated sit-ins outside their homes to publicly shame them. In some cases, the SKS staff physically harassed defaulters, according to the report commissioned by the company. Only in death would the debts be forgiven."[71] Curiously, Unitus stunned the international development sector by promptly closing its doors on 2 July 2010 (less than a month before the IPO) with the bold and rather cryptic message on its website that declared "Mission Accomplished!"[72]

The precise reasons for this abrupt change have not been revealed to the public, leading many people in the industry to scratch their heads, particularly given that less than four months prior to this Unitus had announced an eight-year USD $15 million deal with Citibank and the Overseas Private Investment Corporation.[73] In 2011, a few months after closing its doors, Unitus was resurrected as several different entities operating under the federation umbrella of "Unitus Labs," with the aim of redirecting efforts to financial advisory, equity investing, and supporting livelihood development programs.[74] Although the original Unitus and its successor Unitus Labs are not religious organizations, its leadership has not shifted away from its core membership of Mormons committed to the United Order for building Zion. So, the secrecy surrounding the closing of the original Unitus entity may not be surprising given that the primary criticism levied at the Mormon Church itself (where most practicing members are considered missionaries) is their high level of secrecy and insularity. For example, the finances of the Church have never been made public despite repeated requests over the years. This is an important point; because one of the main bulwarks against criticism of microfinance has been the sector's continued

---

[71] Associated Press, "SKS Under Spotlight in Suicides," *The Wall Street Journal*, 24 February 2012, http://online.wsj.com/article/SB10001424052970203918304577242602296683134.html (accessed 3 January 2014).

[72] The original announcement has been rewritten and the new version now appears on the website of Unitus Labs: United Labs, "Unitus, Inc. Redirects Efforts," 2 July 2010, http://unituslabs.org/updates/unitus-redirects-efforts/ (accessed 3 January 2014).

[73] United Labs, "Unitus Teams Up with OPIC and CITI," 29 March 2010, http://unituslabs.org/updates/unitus-teams-up-with-opic-citi/ (accessed 3 January 2014).

[74] See http://unitus.com/

commitment to transparency at all levels. So, some within the industry have found this entire episode disturbing given the mystery surrounding the changes and the potential it has had to tarnish the reputation of microfinance as an effective model to alleviate poverty.

Another Mormon-led organization, the BYU Center for Economic Self-Reliance (ESR Center), was founded by Todd Manwaring (cofounder of Unitus) in 2003 with the mission of helping families become self-reliant. ESR's inspiration came from the work of Melvin Joseph Ballard, who headed the Church's "Security Plan," an organization established in 1936 to help Mormon families weather the Great Depression.[75] Indeed, Mormons have a long history of welfare programs designed to help other Mormons. In addition to training BYU students[76] as microfinance practitioners, ESR produces training manuals and collaborates with other organizations like Unitus Labs that are working on the ground directly with the poor.[77] Both Ballard and later his grandson, Melvin Russell Ballard were ordained as apostles in the Church, serving as a part of a group of twelve who sit under the presidency within the Mormon hierarchy and whose status as prophets that receive revelations from God is enshrined in Church law.[78] In keeping with the principles of Protestant asceticism, the younger Ballard invoked Benjamin Franklin to support his arguments in a speech he gave on self-reliance and microfinance to the ESR in 2004.[79]

---

[75] BYU Marriott School, "About Melvin J. Ballard," http://marriottschool. byu.edu/selfreliance/about/melvin (accessed 3 January 2014). "Our primary purpose was to set up ... a system under which the curse of idleness would be done away with, the evils of a dole abolished and independence, industry, thrift, and self-respect be once more established amongst our people. The aim of the Church is to help the people to help themselves. Work is to be re-enthroned as the ruling principle of the lives of our Church membership."

[76] According to a 2012 BYU fact sheet, 98.5% of students are affiliated with the Church of Jesus Christ of Latter-day Saints. See: http://yfacts.byu.edu/ Article?id=97.

[77] Sarah Jane Weaver, "Fighting Poverty: Research by BYU's Center for Economic Self-Reliance to Help Poor," *Deseret News* 76, no. 25 (2006), 8–9.

[78] The Church of Jesus Christ of Latter-day Saints, Gospel Library: Gospel Topics, "Prophets," http://www.lds.org/ldsorg/v/index.jsp?locale=0&sourceId =c6549c57af139010VgnVCM1000004d82620a___&vgnextoid=bbd508f5492 2d010VgnVCM1000004d82620aRCRD (accessed 3 January 2014).

[79] Melvin Russell Ballard, "Becoming Self-Reliant—Spiritually and Physically," (address given at Brigham Young University during the opening of the Marriott School's Center for Economic Self-Reliance, Provo, Utah, 11 March 2004).

Manwaring co-authored the book *United for Zion: Principles for Uniting the Saints to Eliminate Poverty* under Unitus Publications. Sold at the ESR bookstore, the book serves as a blueprint for Unitus and lays out the inspiration for its work in microcredit through recounting Mormon history and scripture. Early on, it declares that their spiritual motivation for working with the poor is to bring their souls to Christ.[80] Mormons have historically made little distinction between spiritual and temporal affairs. And in a subtle nod to the notions of the *calling* and *accumulation of wealth* in the Protestant Ethic, the authors recount from the early Mormons, "When people were called on missions (during General Conference, no less!) to mine gold, manufacture iron, grow cotton, or produce silk, they saw it not as degrading of the spiritual but as an elevation of the temporal. These were seen as sacred callings with a spiritual purpose."[81]

In terms of helping the poor through economic development, self-reliance again plays a central role. A chapter of the Unitus book is devoted to equating self-reliance with initiative, drawing inspiration from both Joseph Smith and Brigham Young who saw idlers as a scourge that have the potential of ruining communities. In a bold statement, the authors claim that those who do not take initiative should go hungry.[82] This perspective, however, does not square with the passage above from BYU professor Nibley who interpreted the original message from Christ that the "idle rich shall not eat the bread of the laboring poor."[83] Understandably, the original sentiments expressed by the Church founders were likely meant to inspire a group who needed to pull together for survival at a time when they had little or no outside help. But, this ascetic interpretation can lead to problems when developing microfinance programs targeting the poor as it may not fit other contexts.

The term "initiative" usually means acting before anyone else does. And applying this definition to self-reliance has the potential to set up unfortunate scenarios when working with the poor, who

---

[80] Woodworth, *United for Zion,* 14.
[81] Woodworth, *United for Zion,* 16.
[82] Woodworth, *United for Zion,* 21. See also (Church of Jesus Christ of Latter-day Saints, *The Doctrine and Covenants,* 42:42): "Thou shalt not be idle; for he that is idle shall not eat the bread nor wear the garments of the laborer."
[83] Nibley, *Approaching Zion,* 203–251.

even after receiving a small loan for their business may lack initiative for a variety of reasons such as illness from insufficient food or clean water. The assumption that everyone comes to the table with a level playing field breaks down quickly once people operate outside of a well-ordered society with all of its modern conveniences. Initiative in its strictest sense is simply not possible for many people to achieve when their day is cut short by transportation, medical, and other issues that might thwart them from taking the initiative. So, setting up a rubric that categorizes them as idlers who lack initiative and deserve starvation perpetuates a type of social Darwinism that has the potential to be very destructive as it can strip people down from the social connections they rely upon for survival.

Several other manifestations of the Protestant Ethic are also illustrated throughout the book. For example, in presenting the case for employing cooperative efforts among people engaged in similar businesses, the authors apply similar arguments that Rockefeller made in establishing Standard Oil by recounting the history of a Mormon-run store in the nineteenth century:

> It was a unique idea—to create what would become America's first department store. Until the 1860s when Latter-day Saints launched [Zion's Cooperative Mercantile Institution] ZCMI, U.S. merchants were primarily small firms which each offered a category of products—dresses, shoes, meat, clothes, paper, hardware, and so on. Church leaders saw waste in the proliferation of such stores. Each competed for the same customers, employing too many people in distribution of goods and taking them away from production of goods. ZCMI was created by putting all such products under one giant roof, so to speak.[84]

Similar to refiners under the Standard Oil umbrella, ZCMI's stock *could be* owned by producers and customers. However, as was the case in both entities, there was one major shareholder that controlled everything: Rockefeller for his company and effectively the Mormon Church for theirs. As monopolies, both entities operated as though they were a single individual that was self-reliant. This is very important because it reveals a perhaps uniquely American interpretation of

---

[84] Woodworth, *United for Zion*, 19.

cooperation as merely another form of self-reliance when applied to an insular group. This trap was exactly what Emerson warned people against when he admonished people to be self-reliant by challenging conformity and the status quo. It also raises questions about just how much American involvement in microfinance, particularly when it is fueled by ascetic Protestant influences, is going to be able to help the world's poor over the long term.

Mormon entrepreneurship redefined

In developing a handbook for Mormon small business owners in the Philippines with whom he has worked for several years, Stephen Gibson, a microfinance researcher and professor at BYU, serves as a standout among his peers in recognizing the limitations of entrepreneurship. To help the business owner, Gibson's handbook delineates three distinct business personality types: entrepreneur, manager, and technician. Below are the descriptions he gives for each personality type:

> **Entrepreneur:** Envisions new projects and leads the business. The entrepreneur sees opportunities everywhere, in good times and bad times—often feeling like the rest of the world drags its feet. There is always a new idea just around the corner.

> **Manager:** Plans and organizes the activities of the business. To fulfill that vision, a manager must organize and implement a detailed plan using other people to do the work. The manager often feels frustrated at the entrepreneur who comes in with yet another new idea before s/he has been able to implement yesterday's idea.

> **Technician:** Employs his or her skills to work the plan. S/he is the skilled worker that is constantly "doing it" and thinks that nothing will be done without him or her. S/he may also think that the job will not be done as well as s/he can do it.[85]

These business personality types were first developed by Michael Gerber in his book *The E-Myth Revisited: Why Most Small Businesses*

---

[85] Stephen W. Gibson and Bette M. Gibson, *Where there are No Jobs, Volume 2* (Provo: UT: The Academy for Creating Enterprise, Date Unknown), 9.

Don't Work and What to Do About It.[86] According to Gerber, to some extent most people are a combination of all three; many will achieve success if they cultivate or focus on one of the three roles. One of Gerber's most poignant observations is that most small businesses are started by "technicians" who might lack the requisite skills or temperament to run the business itself. A thriving business requires that these three personality types work in harmony, and wise people will either develop attributes from all three personality types or will find others to join them (as either employees or partners) who are strong in areas where they may be weak.[87]

The holistic livelihood training that Gibson provides helps clients discover what role they can play in the world, and whether they are best suited as an entrepreneur, a manager, a technician, or a laborer. Gibson's departure from the all-clients-as-entrepreneurs perspective also includes a five-person solidarity group model for students to work together to integrate their personality types for the sake of a single business proposal. This can dramatically reduce the kind of alienation caused by an opposition among individuals competing against one another seen in individual models.[88]

---

[86] Michael Gerber, *The E-Myth Revisited: Why Most Small Businesses Don't Work and What to Do About It* (New York: HarperCollins Publishers, Inc., 1995), 1–33.

[87] Gerber, *The E-Myth Revisited,* 1–33.

[88] Although, if done without proper care, this can lead to situations where neighbors are pitted against neighbors.

4
Theology and Development

The previous chapter covered economic development issues rooted in the Protestant Ethic, with a particular focus on American influences in microfinance. This chapter covers issues where theological threads present a more explicit and overt challenge to economic development for the poor. The first section will touch upon issues in microfinance related to religion, gender, and culture. The second section will focus on the Prosperity Gospel and how its view of economic development has challenged the role and authority of traditional African religions. The final section presents a case study on the *bonyads*, religious foundations in the Iranian republic tasked with economic development for the poor. The purpose of the case study is to illuminate drawbacks stemming from state-run, theological economic development programs that lack transparency.

Religion, gender, and culture

In Bangladesh, the Grameen Bank has persistently encountered difficulties in terms of the social and cultural limitations placed on women in Muslim communities. Among their borrowers, ninety seven percent are women, with many living in Muslim households.[1] Muhammad Yunus recounts some of the local customs that have nearly barred him entry into the lives of these women. For example,

---

[1] Grameen Bank, "Grameen Bank at a Glance," http://www.grameen-info. org/index.php?option=com_content&task=view&id=26&Itemid=0 (accessed 31 December 2013).

the custom of *purdah* (literally, "curtain", or "veil") keeps married Muslim women in a state of virtual seclusion from the outside world. He and other Grameen bankers have had to talk to many women through bamboo walls or curtains.[2] As Yunus states, "Even where *purdah* is not strictly observed, custom, family, tradition, and decorum combine to keep relations between women and men in rural Bangladesh extremely formal."[3]

In the early years, instead of asking to enter a woman's house, Yunus would stand in a clearing between several houses, so everyone could see him and observe his behavior. He would wait until a female assistant entered the appointed house and introduce him, shuttling back and forth to answer the potential borrower's questions. Many of these women had never touched money before, leaving those matters to their husbands. Hiding behind veils and even turning their backs, the women displayed tremendous fear of even speaking to Yunus or his loan officers. Everything he offered them was strange and threatening. However, some eventually took a chance and accepted the loans.[4] One key to Grameen's success is its commitment to train loan officers in cultural sensitivity and to negotiate within religious contexts. Critics of Grameen have cited its success as a function of cultural factors that cannot be replicated elsewhere; but Yunus disagrees, saying that not only have they had to struggle *against* culture, but they have also had to create a counterculture that values women's economic contributions.[5]

Among the nearly twelve million microfinance borrowers in Bangladesh, ninety seven percent are female. The worldwide number is around eighty two percent. Why are there so many female clients in societies historically dominated by men? The answer may lie in the motivation for women to take out loans. Many women view loans as a chance not only to overcome poverty through entrepreneurship, but also to help provide for the future of their children. In *The Economics of Microfinance*, authors Armendáriz and Morduch cite evidence from several studies that lending to women yields greater social and economic impacts than lending to men. As one study in Brazil

---

[2] Muhammad Yunus, *Banker to the Poor* (New York: Public Affairs, 2003), 46.

[3] Yunus, *Banker to the Poor*, 74.

[4] Yunus, *Banker to the Poor*, 74–77.

[5] Yunus, *Banker to the Poor*, 111.

reports, "Increasing the bargaining power of women is associated with increases in the share of the household budget spent on health, education and housing as well as improvements in child health."[6] Putting money into the hands of women, rather than their husbands, often ensures that the money will be used for family needs. Indeed, another study concluded that the primary motivation for women to join savings clubs is to protect their money from husbands who routinely squander it on gambling and alcohol.[7] Interestingly, anecdotal evidence from the numerous clients the author has interviewed over the years points towards a general shift in positive relationships between husbands and wives as a result of women's engagement in microfinance. Philosopher and ethicist Martha Nussbaum found similar cases among women's collectives she studied in India. She cites the example of a group of women whom she met in a desert area in the state of Andhra Pradesh who initially resisted joining a collective:

> They thought that it would be a waste of time, changing nothing; and they were afraid that their husbands would react harshly, because the husbands initially told them that the collectives were just an excuse to spend time talking and not working. But over time they began to see that many advantages could be gained by collective discussion and action: now they get the health visitor to come more regularly, they demand that the teacher show up. Men welcome these changes too, and they gain new respect for their wives, seeing them articulating their demands with clarity and winning concessions from local government.[8]

While the peer-lending group models that were discussed in Chapter 2 resolve the need for collateral, these groups also cultivate gender empowerment. As Armendáriz and Morduch state:

> To the extent that group lending in microfinance entails peer monitoring by other borrowers in the same group, microfinance is likely to provide protection to women within their households.

---

[6] Beatriz Armendáriz de Aghion and Jonathan Morduch, *The Economics of Microfinance* (Cambridge, MA: MIT Press, 2005), 190.

[7] Armendáriz de Aghion and Morduch, *The Economics of Microfinance*, 191.

[8] Martha Nussbaum, *Women and Human Development: The Capabilities Approach* (New York: Cambridge University Press, 2000), 43.

In particular, violent acts and abuses by men against women can now be subject to third party scrutiny as peer borrowers will want to find out why a woman in their group has stopped attending repayment meetings. This, in turn, should act as deterrent against domestic violence, and more generally, as an instrument for women to promote their rights and improve their bargaining power vis-à-vis their husbands or other male family members. Rising household incomes in general can also diminish conflicts between husbands and wives by loosening constraints.[9]

In theory, peer-lending groups add protection for female borrowers, but Armendáriz and Morduch also cite studies in Bangladesh that give contradictory results. Two studies report that microfinance in Bangladesh has indeed reduced violence against women, while a third has seen an upsurge in violence caused by exacerbated tensions over who should be the primary income earner in the household.[10]

The story of Kasala, leader of a lending cooperative in India, provides an example of the stress lending groups can have on a family not used to the mother's new role:

I had no time for housework. My husband used to get quite irritated. When he shouted in anger, I used to keep silent. My children miss me at home and feel upset. Seeing that, my husband used to get very upset and sought me to give up the whole thing. But I stuck on. And am happy I did so. However, I feel I lost full control of my household since about two years. I do not really regret. I barely manage cooking at home, rest of the jobs my husband takes care. Though he shouts sometimes, the next day he encourages me to go to the office ... He helps me in planning and executing the logistics for annual meetings and other issues. He drops me off and picks me up in his vehicle when I need to go to neighboring villages when required. He even helps me in depositing amounts in the bank ... I must say that I would not have been able to do all of this if I did not have the support of my family.[11]

---

[9] Armendáriz de Aghion and Morduch, *The Economics of Microfinance*, 192.
[10] Armendáriz de Aghion and Morduch, *The Economics of Microfinance*, 192.
[11] Guy Stuart: "John F Kennedy School of Government Case Study: Women's Thrift Cooperatives in Andhra Pradesh," 2002, 11.

Many microfinance institutions target women because of their perceived credit worthiness, with some having decided to provide financial services exclusively to women. This has triggered an unexpected dilemma within at least one narrow demographic. South Pacific Business Development Foundation (SPBD), a non-profit microfinance institution, provides financial services to women on the island of Samoa.[12] Numerous requests to lend money to *fa'afafines* forced them into a gender debate. *Fa'afafines* are biologically men, but essentially dress and behave like women. SPBD management initially denied these requests, citing their women-only policy. The greatest resistance came from male managers; every female loan officer was willing to revise the policy to accept *fa'afafine*. The general manager ultimately resolved the debate over what defines a man and a woman in this context stating:

> If you act like a woman, you want to be a woman, you dress like a woman, you talk like a woman; therefore, you are a woman and therefore eligible. So for me, why can't *fa'afafine* being transvestite, join in the program? In many ways they are not men. They dress as a woman and do women's duties. The *fa'afafine* are very accepted in society.[13]

Aside from illustrating an anomalous issue in microfinance, this case reveals a trend away from strictly theological debates and towards a variety of issues pertaining to political and economic equality and social justice. Gender and empowerment concerns have been at the forefront of microfinance scholarship since its inception. Now, scholars are examining other social impacts, including how microfinance affects class structure dynamics in places like India.

Caste embeddedness

Guy Stuart, former microfinance lecturer at the Kennedy School at Harvard University, has done extensive research into caste issues within Women's Thrift Cooperatives (WTC) in India. He discovered

---

[12] SBPD also has offices serving the island nations of Fiji, Tonga, and the Solomon Islands.
[13] Regina Galang et al.: "John F Kennedy School of Government Case Study: The Social Construction of Gender: Microfinance and fa'afafines in Samoa." 2005, 1–2.

that "though members of the lowest caste (i.e. Scheduled Caste, formerly known as *Untouchables*) had access to loans once they joined a WTC, they were under-represented in the membership and even more under-represented in the leadership."[14] This presents a potential concern for microfinance institutions that aim to alleviate the poverty of the poorest of the poor. If their target clients are primarily the lowest class Scheduled Caste, why are they reaching out to so few?[15]

The answer lies in the nature of both voluntary group lending and entrenched social norms in Indian societies. Stuart conducted interviews of the Cooperative Development Foundation (CDF), which had introduced the microfinance cooperatives in the district of Andhra Pradesh, India. He also analyzed financial and census data for the district to determine the caste demographics. Stuart found that initially the "CDF tried to promote the involvement of women in existing cooperatives, but found male members of those cooperatives resistant to the idea."[16] CDF resolved gender disputes by promoting new, women-only cooperatives, with a board of directors representative of their membership. Women voluntarily formed peer-lending groups and after two years of close assistance from CDF staff, they began flourishing. Stuart finds strong caste embeddedness in these groups, meaning that they are homogenous from a caste perspective. This separation of castes within groups has ultimately led to excluding Scheduled Caste from leadership of the cooperatives.[17]

---

[14] Stuart, "Women's Thrift", 11. Stuart found that Scheduled Caste members constituted ten percent of the membership of the WTC and received ten percent of the loans. But there was no Scheduled Caste members on the Board of Directors, while forty percent of non-members living in the village were from the Scheduled Castes.

[15] Originating in Hinduism through Vedic scripture, primarily the *Laws of Manu*, the caste system is a social stratification system found primarily in India. The four members of the caste system are: Brahmins (priest caste), Kshatriyas (ruling or military elite caste), Vaishyas (traders and moneylenders), and Shudras (servants). The untouchables were thought to be outside the caste system. While the caste system is illegal in India today, it still forms the basis of many Indian social, political, and economic systems.

[16] Stuart, Guy: "John F Kennedy School of Government Case Study: Caste Embeddedness and Microfinance: Savings and Credit Cooperatives in Andhra Pradesh, India," September 2006, Available at: https://research.hks.harvard.edu/publications/getFile.aspx?Id=230, 13.

[17] Stuart, "Caste Embeddedness," 19–21.

Stuart concluded that CDF challenged the gender embeddedness, but its women-only groups maintained the existing caste structure, especially in terms of leadership. He suggested that this may be because CDF's initial "strategy of gaining access to villages through the existing social hierarchy has had lasting effects on caste background of the presidents of the cooperatives."[18] Although the cooperatives are open to all female villagers, the lower castes may also be under-represented because of their lack of education or inability to comply with the savings rules stipulated by the cooperative.[19] Stuart's argument that gender embeddedness has somehow been resolved by creating women-only cooperatives assumes that gender division is healthy for communities. While it might be true that creating separate cooperatives for women may have been the only option for CDF, the broader question is whether effective community building requires full integration of not only castes but also men and women functioning together.

The Prosperity Gospel and traditional African religions

Much like the country of India, the continent of Africa is a patchwork of diverse cultures whose shared colonialism has left a legacy of dominance and exploitation stamped upon its societies. Much of this exploitation came in the form of the plundering of physical and natural resources by European, North American, and other powers who presented themselves as protectors who came to *civilize* the "savage" continent. This section does not discuss the process by which Africa has been subjugated by foreign powers and their interests. So much has already been written about this long, tragic, and persistent history that serves as a constant reminder that underneath the light of illumination all human beings are capable of possessing a heart of darkness enshrouded in good intentions.

This section is more concerned with *current* African notions of wealth, particularly in Sub-Saharan Africa. Because of African peoples' history of incorporating the ideas of other cultures in which they come into contact, it will examine external ideas that have shaped the thinking of various African cultures. This is particularly the case

---

18   Stuart, "Caste Embeddedness," 32.
19   Stuart, "Caste Embeddedness," 33.

with regard to capitalism's emphasis on credit, which has completely changed the landscape of African economies. The section will provide a sketch of traditional religious and cultural perspectives surrounding the acquisition of and the use of wealth in the African context. In doing so, it will trace a brief history of colonialist influences and the incorporation of external worldviews such as capitalism into African society. It will also include a discussion of how the Pentecostal Prosperity Gospel has reshaped Africa by usurping the authority of traditional rulers and fracturing pluralistic society. Ultimately, the section will argue that the Prosperity Gospel is shifting traditional African notions of wealth, which may thwart their ability to address fundamental issues such as poverty, famine, and violence.

Scholarship and traditional African religions

According to Jacob Olupona, Harvard Professor of African Religious Traditions, because pre-colonial African history has been recounted and recorded primarily by Christian missionaries and other outsiders, much of it carries a bias towards colonialism. In light of this, Olupona has identified four types of scholars who have historically studied African religions, revealing his obvious preference for theologians:

1. **Armchair Scholars:** Many of these people never visited Africa, and based their arguments on secondary sources such as Hegel. Their writings were so persuasive that even today scholars are influenced by their work. The most significant examples were anthropologists, who often started as secret agents, but became scholars. They wanted to write about human sacrifice, because they thought Africans were involved in it; never believing that Africans could have a conception of God. Ultimately, according to Olupona, this scholarship *destroyed* Africa.
2. **Missionaries:** They based their scholarship on the notion that Africans were heathens or idol worshippers and that God is supreme. They wrote extensively about African traditions. They were interested in certain kinds of questions and problems—but primarily interested in something that can be used to critique African religion (i.e. if they could present Africans as unbelievers, they could use it as leverage for conversion).

3. **Theologians:** The most famous of these is the ordained Anglican priest and New Testament scholar, John Mbiti. His book *African Religions and Philosophy* (1969) marked the beginning of the discourse on African philosophy because it challenged Christian assumptions that traditional African religions were demonic and anti-Christian.

4. **Modern Anthropologists:** In an attempt to describe the function of religions, modern anthropologists explain away religion. They deny agency of the sacred, and thus render traditional African religious concepts lifeless.[20]

From the perspective of theologians, it is difficult, if not impossible, to separate African cultures from indigenous African religions, because for many African societies religion is indeed an expression of their culture. This is also true in the case of the spread of both Islam and Christianity, as African culture has successfully internalized and domesticated both of them.[21] In fact, much of Africa's history is a testament to its ability to absorb the influences of external religions and cultures. This makes it difficult to identify an unchanging indigenous African religion because they are not static, but rather eclectic and not based on a fixed doctrine or cosmology.[22] Furthermore, current scholars have begun to reject long-held notions of a unified indigenous African religion and cosmological generalizations attached to African cultures.[23]

For example, many scholars are now challenging the long-held rigid view of Yoruba cosmology in Sub-Saharan Africa as inaccurate. Standard accounts characterize the Yoruba cosmology as a hierarchical pantheon with the sky god, *Olodumare,* reigning over the spiritual and material worlds. Under him are lesser gods, humans, and ancestors. However, this portrayal is based on western conceptions of a pantheon like those found in Ancient Greece and Rome that have been superimposed on the Yoruba cosmology. This distortion

---

[20] From a lecture given by Professor Olupona on 25 September 2008 at Harvard University.

[21] From a lecture given by Professor Olupona on 18 September 2008 at Harvard University.

[22] Lindsay Jones, "African Cosmologies," in *Encyclopedia of Religion*, 2nd ed. (Detroit: Macmillan Reference USA, 2005).

[23] Jones, *African Cosmologies*, 1.

misrepresents the way the Yoruba exercise their religious beliefs and gives the impression that all Yoruba people share the same cosmological views—which they do not.[24]

In light of historical distortions of African cultures and cosmologies, this section will attempt to determine shared views surrounding the acquisition and use of wealth among the African peoples—particularly in Sub-Saharan Africa. While sweeping generalizations can do much harm to this exercise, it is important to remember that in order to arrive at an understanding of pre- and post-colonial African views on wealth, and how external influences continue to shape their ever-changing perspectives, it is important to identify commonalities shared by separate communities. Without discovering common threads in the past and present, one cannot begin the process of deconstructing the forces influencing the future of Africa.

Traditional perspectives on wealth

Given that much of the historical scholarship on the history of Africa often carries a colonialist bias, it is difficult to pin down any historical African views on wealth. Nevertheless, African researchers Ellis and Ter Haar provide a contemporary interpretation that the next few pages will lean heavily upon in order to gain a better understanding of Sub-Saharan African notions of wealth. According to them, money in its modern forms was hardly known before colonial times in some parts of Africa: "Nowhere in pre-colonial Africa had a capitalistic economy in the sense of a pervasive system whereby credit could be obtained through the alienation of property valued in monetary terms." Colonial governments, however, wanted Africans to use money and to pay taxes, but they were also careful to regulate the credit available to them.[25]

Of course, money is not the only type of wealth, and like other cultures, many societies in pre-colonial Africa used some form of wealth as a medium of exchange. In Africa's pre-colonial societies, wealth was classically measured in living beings, able to produce. In the case of herders, this was more likely in the form of animals such as cattle or other beasts. However, in the case of farmers, many

---

[24] Jones, *African Cosmologies*, 3–4.
[25] Stephen Ellis and Gerrie Ter Haar, *Worlds of Power: Religious Thought and Political Practice in Africa* (New York: Oxford University Press, 2004), 118.

transactions consisted in an exchange of wealth involving rights over people. Even today, some societies still observe the practice of paying a bride price for marriage to a fertile woman. Thus, the Atlantic slave trade was quite easily understood as it fit into this system of prices placed on human beings. Interestingly, the large European appetite for slaves meant that some believed that they were actually eating the slaves, as people could find no other explanation.[26]

In terms of acquiring wealth, traditional African attitudes, as one might suspect, often reflect the types of societies where people live. As hunting is widely recognized to contain a spiritual element in forest regions where it remains even today a staple activity, money is often seen as something that needs to be hunted, like a game animal.[27] For example, the diamond digging in Angola, with its risk and uncertainty, resembles a hunting expedition. Congolese men making the trip over the border, with its minefields, and even the diamond-fields themselves represent a dangerous undertaking as teams of diggers "stalk" their mineral quarry.[28]

In this sense, there is a general tendency to consider wealth as natural, to be understood in the same terms as other things that exist in nature. For example, interest is often considered as the offspring of money. In Madagascar, the Malagasy word for interest is *zana-bola*, which means literally "the child of money."[29] As Ellis and Ter Haar point out:

> Similar expressions are to be found in some other African languages, indicating a widespread view that money, like almost everything else in the agrarian economies that dominated Africa until recently, is subject to what are seen as general rules governing nature and fertility. Real wealth in such an environment cannot be produced out of nothing, or merely by multiplying paper, but only through birth, planting, or a similar act of creation. All of these processes are presumed to have an important religious element since they involve the creation of new life.[30]

---

26 Ellis and Ter Haar, *Worlds of Power,* 120–121.
27 Ellis and Ter Haar, *Worlds of Power,* 118.
28 Ellis and Ter Haar, *Worlds of Power,* 119.
29 Ellis and Ter Haar, *Worlds of Power,* 119.
30 Ellis and Ter Haar, *Worlds of Power,* 119–120.

However, this view of money still presents existential problems for even ordinary Africans: "Take the example of the Sudanese cattle-herder who, confused by money's lack of substance like cow's blood and its ability to give birth, asked a visiting anthropologist if it was created by God or man."[31]

With respect to traditional African culture, people do make a distinction on a spiritual level between money and capital. Capital is something that someone can potentially convert into money (e.g. assets like land and buildings). However, "like a spirit, capital is an abstraction, a concept, that may acquire material form."[32] Because capital is not visible like money, it is subject to invisible elements like Adam Smith's "hidden hand" that serves as a mechanism that affects prices in free market transactions. As one African philosopher has noted, "money is itself rather like a traditional medicine in being inherently neither good nor bad. In this respect it could be said that it is also like the traditional spirit world more generally."[33] Africans' recent shift in perspective of spirits as no longer neutral, but having grown evil in nature, might also be said of the invisible nature of capital—especially considering the tremendous capital drain caused by corrupt politicians, which will be discussed in the next few paragraphs.

Wealth, religion, and morality

Despite the absorption of colonial capitalistic ideas and practices, like credit, many African societies today still maintain connections between wealth and the spiritual. While most commercial transactions do not have a spiritual element, some people bargain with the spirit world to receive services. Animal sacrifices are seen as an exchange of life force for the payment of these services—which sometimes may involve the life force of a human being for extraordinary services. This has led to radio and newspaper reports of children

---

[31] Ellis and Ter Haar, *Worlds of Power*, 120, quoted in Sharon E. Hutchison, *Nuer Dilemmas: Coping with money, war and the state* (Berkeley: University of California Press, 1996), 56.
[32] Ellis and Ter Haar, *Worlds of Power*, 116.
[33] Ellis and Ter Haar, *Worlds of Power*, 117, quoted in Joshua N. Kudadjie, *Moral Renewal in Ghana: Ideals, Realities and Possibilities* (Accra: Asempa Publishers, 1995).

being kidnapped and killed to pay a blood debt to a spirit.[34] As Ellis and Ter Haar put it, "massive wealth and power is connected with the manipulation of spiritual forces, and it is supposed that cultivation of these may involve taking the lives of children."[35] Furthermore, the belief of sudden and spectacular wealth is partly rooted in the historical experience of the slave trade.[36]

Many of Africa's corrupt political leaders today cannot be trusted to run their economies effectively in the national interest, especially considering that thirty-nine percent of Africa's capital is thought to be held offshore.[37] Western banks have lent money to Africa, but they have also collaborated in the capital flight that is widely seen as one of the continent's greatest problems.[38] Not only banks cannot be relied upon, but also in an environment that is so poorly regulated it is difficult for the average person to tell the difference between an honest bank and one established simply to defraud people out of their money.[39] These malfeasances by corrupt politicians and dishonest businessmen have continued to keep everyday Africans in a state of abject poverty. In this pervasive atmosphere of financial uncertainty, people try speculative methods of investment such as lotteries and games of chance. According to Ellis and Ter Haar, playing games of chance brings a distinct "religious" element that enters into people's calculations as they try to control the element of risk.[40] As they put it, "a person who believes that the spirit world can be manipulated may be convinced that, with the right technique, he can win the big prize."[41]

This belief in the manipulation of the spirit world lies at the heart of one of the central problems in Africa: political corruption. According to Ellis and Ter Haar, "Politics in Africa today appears to many people as the ultimate form of individual activity, in which power and wealth are conjured out of nothing and used for selfish purposes. Many politicians themselves display a self-belief that is

---

[34] Ellis and Ter Haar, *Worlds of Power*, 122.
[35] Ellis and Ter Haar, *Worlds of Power*, 127.
[36] Ellis and Ter Haar, *Worlds of Power*, 126.
[37] Ellis and Ter Haar, *Worlds of Power*, 132.
[38] Ellis and Ter Haar, *Worlds of Power*, 118.
[39] Ellis and Ter Haar, *Worlds of Power*, 136.
[40] Ellis and Ter Haar, *Worlds of Power*, 133.
[41] Ellis and Ter Haar, *Worlds of Power*, 134.

reckless in the extreme, being prepared to contemplate almost any measure that is calculated to increase their power."[42] Liberian scholar Moses Nagbe points out that these corrupt politicians typically believe that the spirit world will save them from the consequences of their most selfish actions: "God, he believes, will pull a magic formula and all will be improved, without touching his weakness in spending."[43]

Enlisting the power of the spirit world, either to win a lottery or to seize wealth and power occurs at all levels of society. Further compounding corruption problems are that those who are successful in swindling others are "widely admired by young people for their skill and the supposed spiritual power that makes them successful."[44] Even worse, some public servants in Liberia are scorned and ridiculed simply for failing to do the "cultural thing": to exploit the public coffers.[45] Nevertheless, the moral economy of many African peasant cultures still sees the accumulation of wealth as gained at the expense of others.[46] And despite receiving admiration from some of the young, politicians are still seen by most as a "clique of witches, agents of the devil in human form."[47]

Given distrust of government, so many laws lack legitimacy that few Africans show respect for those established by political leaders, even in their own communities. As a result, many Africans are compelled to create new moral bonds, irrespective of the law. To ensure success, and at times even for survival, many people maintain a wide network of personal connections.[48] These networks are a powerful force in African society, and have become an incredible resource for an emerging religious and economic power sweeping the continent: Christianity. Figure 4.1 is from a 2010 Pew Research report tracing the growth of both Christianity and Islam in Sub-Saharan Africa, revealing remarkable shifts over the past century.

---

[42] Ellis and Ter Haar, *Worlds of Power,* 154.
[43] Ellis and Ter Haar, *Worlds of Power,* 155, quoted in K. Moses Nagbe, "Liberia: A Land of the Magic God," *Daily Observer* [Monrovia], 10, 76, and 12 June 1990.
[44] Ellis and Ter Haar, *Worlds of Power,* 135.
[45] Ellis and Ter Haar, *Worlds of Power,* 157.
[46] Ellis and Ter Haar, *Worlds of Power,* 120.
[47] Ellis and Ter Haar, *Worlds of Power,* 154.
[48] Ellis and Ter Haar, *Worlds of Power,* 162.

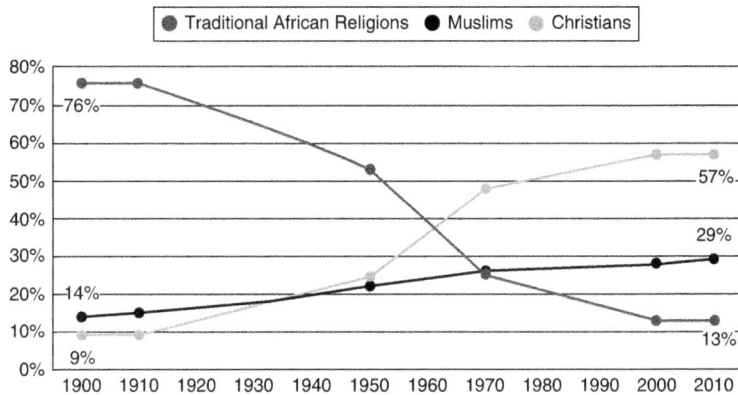

Figure 4.1 Growth of Islam and Christianity in Sub-Saharan Africa since 1900[49]

Source: World Religion Database. Historical data draw on government records, historical atlases and reports of religious organizations at the time. Later figures drew on U.N. population estimates, surveys and censuses (Pew Forum on Religion & Public Life, April 2010)

While Christianity has been embedded in Africa for centuries, both influencing and being absorbed by African culture, new religious movements such as Pentecostal, Charismatic, and Evangelical Christianity have been usurping the role of traditional spiritual leaders and governing the relationship between the spirit and the material worlds. The same Pew Research Center report puts the total number of these three strands of Christianity at eight hundred and seventy million (roughly thirty five percent of African Christians).[50] As a note, Latin America has seen similar growth trends in the spread of these movements where nearly thirty percent of the population identified as evangelical in a landscape long dominated by

---

[49] Pew Research Center, "Tolerance and Tension: Islam and Christianity in Sub-Saharan Africa," 15 April 2010, http://www.pewforum.org/2010/04/15/executive-summary-islam-and-christianity-in-sub-saharan-africa/ (accessed 4 January 2014).

[50] Pew Research Center, "Christian Movements and Denominations," 19 December 2011, http://www.pewforum.org/2011/12/19/global-christianity-movements-and-denominations/ (accessed 4 January 2014).

Catholicism.[51] While these groups preach the message of converting people to follow Jesus Christ, the principal message many of them bring is the "Prosperity Gospel." For poor people suffering from economic oppression, the idea that they can become rich by following certain principles is quite attractive. Reverend Samuel Abogunrin, Professor of New Testament Studies at the University of Ibadan in Nigeria, provides the following summary of the central message of the Prosperity Gospel:

> If you come to Jesus he will save you, give you all you want, including good health, make you rich and successful; and free you once and for all from poverty and disease. The chief product of what is offered is the "new you", instead of the "new life" in Jesus Christ.[52]

Abogunrin believes that the Prosperity Gospel is deeply rooted in Gnostic teachings and principles, along with some aspects of Buddhism and Hinduism. He adds, "The teachings in Nigeria have also been greatly influenced by belief in destiny, predestination as taught in African Traditional Religion." By placing more emphasis on following specific principles, guidelines, techniques and formulas both to achieve success and for one to discover who he is, he deems this a form of spiritual arrogance.[53] Nevertheless, Ellis and Ter Haar point out that this is not entirely new in either Africa or even the rest of the world:

> People in many historical periods and in most places, including Europe and North America, have perceived there to be a connection between religion and economic fortunes. Specifically in regard to Africa, the idea that prosperity has a mystical aspect, and that its roots are in the spirit world, predates the continent's

---

[51] Pew Research Center, "Overview: Pentecostalism in Latin America," 5 October 2006, http://www.pewforum.org/2006/10/05/overview-pentecostalism-in-latin-america/ (accessed 4 January 2014).

[52] Samuel O. Abogunrin (Gen. Editor), J.O. Akao, D.O. Akintunde, D. Kunle, G.N. Toryough and P.A. Oguntoye (2007) (Eds) *Biblical Studies and Corruption in Africa*. Biblical Studies Series No.6. Ibadan: NABIS, p. 654.

[53] Abogunrin, "Jesus' Pronouncements on Wealth," 271.

current economic problems by hundreds of years, at least as far as historical records allow us to judge. Techniques for communicating with the spirit world have changed constantly during that time, although the basic idea of using spiritual resources to sustain material life has remained. In that sense the "Prosperity Gospel," or radical forms of Islam, or even rumors about human body-parts being used to acquire wealth and power, are simply recent or not-so-recent adaptations of much older beliefs that have often assimilated ideas from outside.[54]

This reliance on the Prosperity Gospel has generated two major problems. The first is that the doctrine fails to make any distinction between needs and wants. While many religious people may not find too much fault with the argument that God might bestow blessings on faithful adherents, it is a stretch to assume that God will also satisfy a spectrum of lust and desires. According to Abogunrin, the preachers of the health and wealth gospel (as it is also known) have, perhaps intentionally, mistranslated the Greek word for need ($\chi\rho\epsilon\iota\alpha$) as "new houses, fancy cars (and you can actually decree what brand and color you want), expensive clothing, and enough cash in order to live like kings, since we are royal sons and daughters, and kings and queens in the real sense."[55]

The basic message of the Prosperity Gospel is that God will free all believers from sickness and material poverty: giving them health and wealth in exchange for their conversion and obedience. According to its proponents, God wants the faithful to be rich. This is what Jim Bakker taught for many years in America, until he was imprisoned for fraud and while in his prison cell recanted his own teachings as contrary to what Jesus was trying to convey in the gospels about wealth. His book entitled *I Was Wrong* is a testament to his conversion away from the Prosperity Gospel and its belief that religious belief will bring people material wealth.[56] As Bakker discovered, the Prosperity Gospel establishes an anthropomorphic relationship that is both personal and conditional with one's higher power who takes the form of a kind of cosmic Santa Claus.

---

[54] Ellis and Ter Haar, *Worlds of Power,* 180.
[55] Abogunrin, "Jesus' Pronouncements on Wealth," 272.
[56] See Jim Bakker and Ken Abraham, *I was wrong* (Nashville: T. Nelson, 1996).

Eventually, cognitive dissonance effectively cuts people off from their higher power as each person continually measures his or her faith by outward appearances that may never resemble the image of personal and spiritual success.

However, proponents of the Prosperity Gospel tell a different story. Pentecostal leader Ogbu Kalu has said that in terms of poverty the first task of Christianity is "to save people from hopelessness by creating new tools of empowerment and new sources of security, not by repeating the old excuses about suffering as a sign of being like Christ."[57] He defines a broader definition of the gospel than Abogunrin:

> Prosperity goes beyond material wealth to cover such matters as spiritual renewal of relationship with God in Christ through the power of the Holy Spirit, health, reversal of economic desolation and political and social well-being of individuals and communities. Prosperity is a function of repentance and renewal of a relationship which had been broken by sin and pollution; it is also a sign that healing has occurred. The process involves both repentance and claiming of promises in the bible. Objectors to the faith-word movement point to insufficient recognition of the sovereignty and freedom of God.[58]

It is easy to see how powerfully this message resonates with people stricken down by disease and/or trapped in a state of poverty. For them, it is not about being rich, but about being human and having the kind of life that others might take for granted. Furthermore, the Prosperity Gospel might also tap into the belief that wealth and abundance need to be sought after, to be *hunted*—although, this time not out in the forest, but rather in one's own self-discovered heart and connection to God.

The second problem with the emergence of the Prosperity Gospel is that by diminishing the authority of traditional African leaders (aided by a dysfunctional and corrupt state), it threatens the diversity of religious traditions. As Olupona points out, "they can no longer provide the sacred canopy under which robust African pluralism existed

---

[57] Ogbu Kalu, *Power, Poverty, and Prayer: The Challenges of Poverty and Pluralism in African Christianity, 1960–1996* (Frankfurt: Peter Lang GmbH, 2000), 127.
[58] Kalu, *Power, Poverty, and Prayer*, 127.

for centuries."[59] Olupona also strongly argues that the demand by Pentecostal and evangelical groups for converts to divorce themselves from traditional worldviews is doing violence to African people and societies. He observes some communities reacting negatively to the Prosperity Gospel—seeing famine and violence as the real enemies:

> Rather than retreating into self-help mantras, they are engaging in food banks, peasant cooperatives, and neighborhood watches. These communities have recognized that peace is only possible with cooperation across barriers – that there is no good life to be gotten from anything less than hard work and engagement.[60]

Olupona correctly identifies the aim of some in the Pentecostal Prosperity Gospel movement to replace traditional African cultural leaders. Indeed, Kalu boldly asserts that the Pentecostal "message of God's promises of prosperity has been an empowerment and tool of hope, contradicting the rulers."[61]

Religious leaders like Kalu believe that African leaders, traditional or otherwise, have let Africa down (an argument and a worldview not restricted to Africa alone). From their perspective, the Prosperity Gospel offers the poor a way out of their desperate situation, and this cannot happen without eliminating the fractious elements caused by western notions of pluralism. He does not call for the end of inter-faith dialog, but rather a halting to what he considers the manipulation of religious allegiances by corrupt nation states and other power-seekers.[62] However, Kalu may have overlooked the ambitious power-seekers within his own movement, who critics believe somewhat resemble the political "clique of witches" they seek to replace. For instance, Abogunrin contends that many of these church leaders are involved in the same kind of fraudulent practices for which Nigeria's political leaders are well known:

> For example about two years ago a young hotel worker stole millions of Naira from his employers and donated this to one

---

[59] Jacob Olupona, "On Africa, A Need for Nuance," *Harvard Divinity Bulletin,* Autumn 2007, 41.

[60] Olupona, "On Africa," 41.

[61] Kalu, *Power, Poverty, and Prayer,* 127.

[62] Kalu, *Power, Poverty, and Prayer,* 135.

of the prosperity churches in Lagos for the purpose of becoming "multi-multi millionaire." He was arrested and he confessed that he donated the money to the Church in order to receive a hundred fold from God. The church leader agreed that the church received the money and that it was a voluntary donation. The Church leader refused to return the stolen money because the donor was not forced to do so. His relations based in the USA had to pay the money back in order to prevent the young man from going to jail. The matter was published in The News Magazine, Vol. 26, No. 23 of 19 June 2006. Several news papers had published the matter before then. That church is yet to refund the stolen money given as offering. There are matters that are worse than this, relating to moral matters and probity. There is hardly any week that similar matters do not appear in the dailies or periodicals.[63]

The need for new leadership

By shifting the focus of wealth accumulation away from communities and onto the self, the Prosperity Gospel and its proponents are undermining Africans' ability to return to their root values and unite in helping one another. However, one cannot place the blame squarely on the shoulders of religious leaders in these movements. Post-colonial political rulers squandered their chances to reclaim Africa and to raise its people to a standard of living equal to the continent's resources and passions. While churches stood by, and at times aided these corrupt politicians, the rest of the world watched and even participated in the destruction of African society. Can we really blame poor people for turning to others who offer them hope in times of desperation?

The question is how the new leaders, whether they be political, religious, academic, or otherwise, can create a healthy roadmap for change. Furthermore, how can people on the outside support their neighbors, both near and far, without becoming ensnared in typical Lord Jim or Christ-complex traps?[64] William Easterly, a long-time economist at the World Bank and ardent critic of current

---

[63] Abogunrin, "Jesus' Pronouncements on Wealth," 276.

international development policies, argues that the commonplace call for more education and international development money is misguided. Instead, he calls for reforming corrupt African governments and instituting greater regulatory information disclosure, in banking and at all levels of government.[65] This is something also supported by Paul Collier, author of *The Bottom Billion*, mentioned in Chapter 2.[66] "Big Planners" (as Easterly refers to them, taking aim at world renowned economist and author of *The End of Poverty*, Jeffrey Sachs) develop huge schemes to try to help Africa—schemes that ultimately do not work. What Africa needs, he suggests, is for donors to support small-scale projects developed by people he calls "Searchers."

Easterly criticizes Planners as academics who design utopian models that take years to implement, while Searchers are typically local people who use common sense approaches to solve their own problems rather than programs that often lead to corrupt politicians lining their pockets.[67] Furthermore, the $2.3 trillion spent on foreign aid programs over the past five decades has done little to tackle poverty and one of the biggest killers in Africa: malaria.[68] He underscores the work in Malawi by the nonprofit Population Services International (PSI) as a positive example of a Searcher. Driven by local representatives, PSI channeled grant funding into selling insecticide-treated

---

[64] Joseph Conrad's novel *Lord Jim* is the fictionalized account of a young British naval officer who commits an act of cowardice while at sea and attempts self-redemption by setting out to protect a small tribe in a remote jungle. In the end, Jim's desire to redeem himself through heroism falls apart when he stumbles as a result of his lingering character defects, and chooses death as a last resort at self-sacrifice. Many of Conrad's stories follow themes where colonialists seek to "civilize" presumably "primitive" societies, but wind up exposing their own ignorance and hubris.

[65] William Easterly, *White Man's Burden: Why the West's Efforts to Aid the Rest Have Done So Much Ill and So Little Good* (New York: Penguin Books, 2006), 375.

[66] As noted in Chapter 2, Collier gives four main reasons why countries are caught in what he refers to as a *development trap*: poor governance, close proximity to unstable countries, internal conflict and civil war, and issues related to natural resources.

[67] Easterly, *White Man's Burden*, 383.

[68] Easterly, *White Man's Burden*, 4.

bed nets to mothers through Malawi antenatal clinics for fifty cents a net. Within four years, the nationwide average of children under five years old (among the highest at risk for contracting malaria) using bed nets rose from eight to fifty five percent. By contrast, a bed net giveaway program in Zambia during the same time period found that forty percent of recipients did not use the bed nets.[69] This example reinforces the need to channel funding to local representatives and, wherever possible, employ a pay-for-service model that ensures stakeholder acceptance. Another example can be taken from the discussion of Accumulating Savings and Credit Associations (ASCAs) in Chapter 2. As was mentioned, one of the ASCA model's greatest achievements is people learning to come together to manage wealth and to direct it in ways that help one another and the communities where they live. No large-scale planning or development projects are needed for these to be a healthy and powerful force of wealth creation and management in the communities.

Of course, this cannot work unless the world community makes a solid commitment to punish corruption out of existence—which could be accelerated through bypassing governments wherever possible and directing funding to local programs that work. It is not an easy task, but here is where the churches can be most effective. Rather than focusing on conversion and luring people away from their communities, religious leaders can help communities come together for the larger task of holding their government officials accountable. From a Christian perspective, this was arguably one of Christ's primary undertakings. The question is whether African religious leaders, traditional or otherwise, are themselves up to the same task.

Case study: the Iranian *bonyads*

The *bonyads* of Iran continually threaten Ayatollah Khomeini's vision for "one voice" (*vahdat-e kalameh*). His call to Muslim unity that initially fueled the Islamic Revolution in 1980 soon led to political factions for a variety of economic, political, and social reasons. While radicals, populist-statists, and conservatives struggled for power in the aftermath of the revolution, semi-public charitable

---

[69] Easterly, *White Man's Burden*, 13–14.

foundations, known as *bonyads*, run by clerics and answerable only to the Ayatollah, began entrenching themselves into all aspects of Iranian economy and society.

Over the years, the *bonyads* have grown in size (primarily using government funds acquired through taxation) to such an extent that some are now more powerful than the government of Iran. This has led many critics to question why these massive organizations, some of which control entire industries, do not have government oversight. Recent government attempts to force *bonyads* to become more transparent have proven difficult and in some cases have failed completely—a testament to the tremendous influence these organizations wield.

This section will review the history of these mysterious organizations that engage in everything from charity for the poor, supporting Iranian filmmakers, building mosques, operating textile plants, and producing soft drinks, to financing terrorist operations. It will also review recent attempts by the government to regulate them—since over the last thirty years some of them have grown to become powerful international conglomerates with almost no accountability to the public. Because of the secretive nature of these organizations, little information is available in order to determine their level of corruption, if any. Suzanne Maloney, a Senior Fellow at the Brookings Institute and author of the 2008 book *Iran's Long Reach: Iran as a Pivotal State in the Muslim World* is a leading scholar of Iran who has done much to lift back the curtain on the *bonyads*. Ultimately, this section will argue for increased support among the Iranian populace to put pressure on the *bonyads* to open their doors to government oversight and regulation. Without proper management, these organizations will both continue to drain Iran's resources away from the people who need it most and prevent Iran from becoming a leading economic force in the world. Of course, given the persistent political climate of repression of the populace in Iran, this may not be feasible.

History of the charitable foundations

Islamic-based charitable foundations (*vaaf* in Arabic) have been around for a millennium, serving as a means for investing state money into charity programs and to provide for the financial independence of the religious hierarchy. The term *vaaf* is often translated as "inalienable endowment," which is appropriate considering these foundations are created using bequeathed property, land or assets to religious institutions.[70] Throughout the Muslim world, the endowments have "financed the construction and development of mosques, shrines, religious schools, universities, hospitals and other charitable endeavors, serving as the primary mechanism for large-scale savings and capital investment."[71] Beginning in sixteenth-century Iran, "emerging conceptualizations of property rights and the religiosity of the ruling dynasty greatly expanded the scope of these religious foundations, and since that time, the relative security of *vaaf* endowments in Iran provided the clergy with 'economic independence' from the state and thus enabled them to remain aloof from politics, unlike their counterparts in the Arab world."[72]

After World War I, Ataturk, in an attempt to modernize his newly created state of Turkey, nationalized all of the *vaaf* along with abolishing the state structures associated with the Ottoman caliphate. This process happened earlier in neighboring Afghanistan, where in 1896 most religious endowments were eliminated and their assets placed under direct control of the government. In Iran, however, where religious leaders jealously guarded these institutions, the process of government intervention and oversight moved much slower.[73]

It was not until Reza Shah Pahlavi (ruler of Iran from 1925 to 1941) and his reformist policies designed to modernize the country that the *vaaf* came under government scrutiny. However, for the first part of the twentieth century, the social and political power of the Iranian clergy meant that even Reza Shah "could not afford to fully alienate the religious leadership by taking them on directly over the issue of endowments."[74] His son, Mohammad Reza Shah Pahlavi (ruler of Iran from 1941 to 1979), proved more successful in limiting the power of the clergy, specifically by weakening their organizational structures. As part of a gradual secularization process, the younger Shah passed educational reforms in 1949 that established an institutional competitor to the seminary system. Furthermore, the land reform program

---

[70] Suzanne Maloney, "Politics, Patronage, and Social Justice: Parastatal Foundations and Post-Revolutionary Iran," Ph.D. Dissertation (The Fletcher School of Law and Diplomacy, 2001), 183.

[71] Maloney, "Politics, Patronage, and Social Justice," 183.

[72] Maloney, "Politics, Patronage, and Social Justice," 185.

[73] Maloney, "Politics, Patronage, and Social Justice," 188.

[74] Maloney, "Politics, Patronage, and Social Justice," 189.

drafted in 1959 (and finally implemented in 1962) enraged the clergy, who united against him for the primary reason that it failed to exempt properties held by the *vaaf* as part of the land distribution process.[75] Over the next twenty years the Shah established greater control over the administration of the *vaaf* and marginalized the clergy as he slowly concentrated and consolidated his power of the country and its institutions. In 1964, he created an independent agency, the Endowments Organization (*Sazman-e Awqaf*), from the department within the Ministry of Culture to regulate the *vaaf*. The Endowments Organization, under the supervision of the Prime Minister's office, made common use of *vaaf* properties to friends of the Shah, and placed secular leaders (and even those connected to SAVAK[76]) in charge of these sacred institutions. Most troubling was not only the greater central control over the *vaaf*, but that the monarchy "increasingly ceased to recognize any distinction between the assets bequeathed to them over the years and the resources of the state."[77]

In 1958, the Shah established a foundation in his own name. As Maloney points out, the Pahlavi foundation was partly philanthropic and party propagandistic:

> Despite authentic programs of charitable giving and investment in the development of the nation, the larger mission of the Pahlavi Foundation was as a vehicle for the accumulation of royal family wealth and, to a lesser extent, as a promotional vehicle for the family's prestige and patronage, as well as those Iranians close to the royal family.[78]

The Foundation controlled Bank Omran, the country's fifth largest bank, along with several other Iranian banks (an estimated fifteen percent of the commercial lending market) and insurance

---

[75] Maloney, "Politics, Patronage, and Social Justice," 191.

[76] SAVAK stands for *Sazeman-i Ettelaat va Amniyat-i Keshvar* and was officially the Shah's National Organization for Intelligence and Security. Receiving a great deal of assistance from the CIA, SAVAK operated an extensive network of informants that spied on Iranian citizens. It was officially dissolved by Khomeini shortly after he came to power in 1979.

[77] Maloney, "Politics, Patronage, and Social Justice," 193.

[78] Maloney, "Politics, Patronage, and Social Justice," 200.

companies.[79] Naturally, the Pahlavi Foundation became a particular target by revolutionary critics as a symbol of the Pahlavi family's excesses. It was "widely and cynically regarded as a corrupt organization, a convenient slush fund for the Shah and the parasites surrounding him. This political reality was more important than the precise truth of the matter."[80]

No longer the Shah's foundations

Starting in mid-September 1978, general strikes and other revolutionary activities aimed at taking control of the day-to-day functioning of every single one of the Shah's government institutions and entities. The situation in large factories, banks, corporations, and companies belonging to the private sector was not much different from that of the government.[81] During this period, Khomeini selected a group of about fifteen people, known as the Revolutionary Council, charged with the task of planning for the Post-Revolution era. They were initially the highest decision-making body, assuming the power to run the country, and to chart its future. Before Khomeini dissolved the Revolutionary Council in July 1980 when the new Majiles held its first session, they passed more than sixty resolutions, decrees, and ordinances, whereby ownership of many large private corporations and companies was transferred to the new government.[82]

As one might suspect, the new regime dissolved many of the institutions conceived by the Shah as vehicles for his political, personal, or cultural goals. The Pahlavi Foundation and its assets were seized by the new government, and some of these assets transferred to the foundations, some new and some formerly *vaaf*, inside the new religious infrastructure—such as the *Bonyad-e Mostazafan va Janbazan* (Foundation of the Oppressed and Self-Sacrificers) and *Bonyad-e Shahid* (Martyrs' Foundation). Maloney points out how the *bonyads* fit into the new Islamic Republic:

> Emblematic in both name and stated mission of the redistributive and idealized character of the Islamic Revolution, the *bonyads*

---

[79] Maloney, "Politics, Patronage, and Social Justice," 213.

[80] Anthony Parsons, *The Pride and the Fall: Iran, 1974–1979* (London: Jonathon Cape, 1984), 29.

[81] Thierry Coville, *The Economy of Islamic Iran: Between State and Market* (Louvain: Institut Français de Recherche en Iran, 1994), 45.

[82] Coville, *The economy of Islamic Iran*, 46.

exemplify one of the core ideological innovations of the revolution's architect, Ayatollah Ruhollah Khomeini – the amalgamation of religious imagery with a populist, class-rooted appeal that deliberately targeted a broad array of socioeconomic groups. Hence, these organizations which operate in the name of the "dispossessed" and the "martyrs" have, in practice, developed into conglomerates oriented toward capital accumulation, with their proclaimed ideological objectives distinctly subordinate, though never fully subsumed.[83]

However, Maloney reminds us that the term *bonyad* implies nothing more than the English term "foundation," and indeed, "many of the organizations which incorporate this term in their name do not substantially differ from corresponding institutions in other countries."[84] Therefore, when people discuss the "problem of the *bonyads*" in Iran, it can cause confusion given that the country has literally hundreds of *bonyads* operating within its borders—the vast majority of which are either non-profit organizations or simply research institutions. For example, the Farabi Foundation grants government subsidies to support the Iranian cinema industry,[85] maintaining a seemingly innocuous cultural-based mission, while the *Bonyad-e Panzadah-e Khordad* (fifteenth of Khordad Foundation) "gained international notoriety in 1989, with a pledge of a $2 million bounty to anyone who would implement Khomeini's fatwa condemning author Salman Rushdie to death for apostasy."[86]

Despite having differing agendas that preclude them from wholesale scrutiny based on their objectives, *bonyads* do share some common characteristics. Nearly all of them are run by clerics, and most of their initial financing (at least the ones established post-Revolution) came through the assets of the Shah, his ruling elite, and other Iranians who fled the country after the revolution. These included hundreds of companies in all sectors of the economy. As Kanovsky argues, "The *bonyads* are supposed to use profits from these

---

[83] Maloney, "Politics, Patronage, and Social Justice," 14.

[84] Maloney, "Politics, Patronage, and Social Justice," 215.

[85] Farabi Cinema Foundation, http://www.fcf.ir/en/ (accessed 2 January 2014).

[86] Maloney, "Politics, Patronage, and Social Justice," 212.

enterprises to provide inexpensive housing, healthcare, and other social services to the poor. In reality, much of it is siphoned off by those in control and relatively little reaches the needy."[87]

In fact, Abdolhassan Banisadr, Iran's first post-Revolution president became alarmed by the power of *bonyads*. He complained to Ayatollah Khomeini in 1980 about their rampant corruption, urging him to bring them under formal government control. According to Banisadr, the regime never took this seriously and consequently the free rein given to *bonyads* allowed "the mullahs to set up a parallel state." Islam as a galvanizing force "finished a long time ago," he says. "Now it is all about money."[88]

Over the years, other critics have also complained that the *bonyads* lack general government oversight. This has become a central issue in both national politics and economics for while the *bonyads* control an estimated twenty percent of Iran's GDP, according to Afshin Molavi, an expert on the Iranian economy, the clerics who run them "jealously guard their books from prying eyes."[89] The most prominent, the Foundation for the Oppressed and Disabled, for example, "controls 20% of the country's production of textiles, 40% of soft drinks, two-thirds of all glass products and a dominant share also in tiles, chemicals, tires, foodstuffs. Some economists argue that its chair – and not the Minister of Finance or president of the central bank – is considered the most powerful economic post in Iran."[90] In fact, the IMF (International Monetary Fund) has suggested that the foundation be classified as a holding company rather than a philanthropic organization.[91] Maloney points out something more disturbing:

> The foundations are largely unaccountable to the government (although they are directly responsible to the Faqih, or spiritual

[87] Eliyahu Kanovsky, *Iran's Economic Morass: Mismanagement and Decline under the Islamic Republic,* Policy papers; no. 44 (Washington, DC: Washington Institute for Near East Policy, 1997).

[88] Andrew Higgins, "Inside Iran's Holy Money Machine," *The Wall Street Journal,* 2 June 2007, http://online.wsj.com/news/articles/SB118072271215621679 (accessed 5 January 2014).

[89] Afshin Molavi, *The Soul of Iran* (New York: Norton, 2005), 176.

[90] Molavi, *The Soul of Iran,* 176.

[91] International Monetary Fund, "Islamic Republic of Iran: Staff Report for the 2004 Article IV Consultation," IMF Country Report 04/306 (Washington, DC, September 2004), 46.

leader of the nation), enabling them to avoid taxation and full disclosure of their activities. This exemption tacitly sanctions the bonyads' intervention in both domestic and international politics on behalf of a distinct and independent agenda that, at times, contravenes that of the government itself.[92]

Maloney also mentions that not only is there little written about these enigmatic organizations (aside from commentaries in the media and scholarly works), but that some Iranians actually consider them too dangerous to endeavor a thorough investigation.[93] This may be among the myriad reasons why the *bonyads* have evaded formal public investigations into their activities. However, given the recent plunge in oil prices and the general financial erosion of the global economy, these organizations may no longer enjoy their protected status. Iranians, whose wealth has certainly shrunk over the years, will certainly want to know where their taxes are going, and eventually they will turn their eyes on the *bonyads*, no matter how much potential danger these actions entail.

Occasional brief glimmers of hope

The 2005 election of Khatami as president of Iran ushered in a brief moment of public hope for a new Iran. As was pointed out earlier, the *bonyads* sometimes run counter to government interests. Furthermore, some critics have also noticed that their losses have imposed substantial costs on the Iranian budget and the economy in general.[94] Molavi underscores the recent political struggle in how to deal with the *bonyads*:

> Technocrats in the Central Bank and surrounding President Khatami have called for the breakup of the bonyads, but powerful bazaar merchants and senior conservative clergy resist. The current closed economic system, with its convoluted, corrupt avenues of horse trading, benefits the merchant with state connections and the official willing to take a cut of the deal. Iranian

---

[92] Maloney, "Politics, Patronage, and Social Justice," 15.

[93] Maloney, "Politics, Patronage, and Social Justice," 18–19.

[94] Keith Crane, Rollie Lal, and Jeffrey Martini, *Iran's Political, Demographic, and Economic Vulnerabilities* (Arlington, VA: Rand Corporation, 2008), 81.

officials have taken note, making the combating of corruption the centerpiece of their political discourse, though few meaningful steps have been taken to change the system. The outcome of this battle may be as important to the future of Iran as the raging political battle over reform, because it could mean a spark of life to Iran's stagnant economy.[95]

Indeed, under the Khatami presidency, "a number of economic policy changes were introduced to create a more-level playing field among state-owned enterprises, the *bonyads*, and the private sector."[96] In addition to forcing some of the *bonyads* to begin paying taxes, Parliament passed a law stipulating that they were under the "supervision of the president and the auspices of the supreme leader." This led to the brother of the head of the Oppressed Foundation being convicted of embezzlement.[97] It should be noted, however, that although these reforms diminished their access to subsidies, *bonyads* still retained preferential access to loans. The Ahmadinejad government brought about a regression in some of the reforms of Khatami and his predecessors. However, since the *bonyads* maintain considerable holdings and answer only to Iran's supreme leader, Ayatollah Ali Khamenei, it means that the government subsidy reforms may have had very little effect on their operations.

Thwarting another revolution through transparency

Saeed Laylaz, a prominent economist in Iran, compares his country's situation to that of medieval Europe, "where the wealth of the Roman Catholic Church and its claim to speak for God allowed popes and cardinals to rival and often eclipse kings. 'Religion and economics are always together everywhere', says Mr. Laylaz. Without cash, he says, clerics 'just become mystics.'"[98] Maloney offers a slightly sympathetic view of the ramifications of the *bonyads*:

> The *bonyads* have insulated the Islamic Republic from some of the challenges emanating from an autonomous society under the

---

[95] Molavi, *The Soul of Iran*, 177.
[96] Crane et al., *Iran's Political, Demographic, and Economic Vulnerabilities,* 82.
[97] Higgins, "Inside Iran's Holy Money Machine."
[98] Higgins, "Inside Iran's Holy Money Machine."

monarchy. They have also vested tremendous financial, political and symbolic assets in institutions which lie beyond the reach of the state and which have been sacralized with the imprimatur of religious authority. Thus, they have contributed to the longevity of the Islamic Republic, but they have also laid the foundations for on-going resistance to its authority.[99]

Despite possibly contributing to the longevity of the Islamic Republic, the lack of transparency in the *bonyads*, and in Iran in general, presents long-term problems not only for fighting corruption, but also for the well-being of the nation's economy. As journalist and frequent writer on Iran Dr Abbas Bakhtiar notes, "Corruption increases inefficiencies and hampers economic growth. Corruption eats at the social fabric of the society, changing people's perception of important values such as honesty, loyalty and hard work ... Lack of financial regulations has allowed people to amass fortunes without anyone asking how these people have earned so much money in such a short time."[100] In addition to the *bonyads*, other important sectors such as the traditional Bazaars also operate without proper supervision and regulations. "There are virtually millions of people who do not pay taxes and hence operate outside the formal economy."[101]

Transparency International ranked Iran 133 out of 176 countries in its Corruption Perceptions Index in 2012 (Denmark, with the lowest perceived corruption, ranked 1st).[102] Ranking behind such countries as Nigeria, Pakistan, and the Ukraine—countries widely known as corrupt—has hampered Iran's ability to attract foreign investment. The series of post-Revolution presidents have been unable to control the system of *bonyads* that have grown into international conglomerates, some of which allegedly finance terrorist organizations such as Hezbollah in Lebanon. Nevertheless, continued and increasing pressure by both the government and the democratic populace may ultimately help to bring them under the transparency umbrella and lead to their reform.

---

[99] Maloney, "Politics, Patronage, and Social Justice," 362.

[100] Abbas Bakhtiar, "Ahmadinejad's Achilles Heel: The Iranian Economy," 25 January 2007, *Payvand's Iran News*, http://www.payvand.com/news/07/jan/1295.html#_edn7 (accessed 4 January 2014).

[101] Bakhtiar, "Ahmadinejad's Achilles Heel."

[102] Transparency International, "Corruption Perceptions Index 2012," http://cpi.transparency.org/cpi2012/results/ (accessed 2 January 2014).

However, this would require a shift away from societal corruption, one that might only come about through a massive paradigm shift brought on either by an economic crisis or worse, through another revolution.

***

This chapter has examined topics where theological perspectives and their cultural expressions present legitimate challenges, and even barriers to alleviating poverty through economic development. The first section explored the friction caused when microfinance confronts the traditional role of women and conservative cultural norms rooted in religion. Indeed, microfinance institutions primarily target women for their credit worthiness and the promise of helping a household contribute to the long-term health and success of its children. Women's empowerment, by its very definition, represents a threat to the power dynamic of a family where the *perceived* power shift runs counter to conservative religious expectations. Aside from a slow and steady approach to raising awareness in communities and families on a case-by-case basis, there is no easy resolution to the quagmire microfinance has stepped into. The case of the *Fa'afafines* of Samoa not only symbolizes the difficulty of trying to maintain a strict policy of serving only female clients, but it also raises questions about whether or not women should remain the primary target of microfinance. Perhaps it will be a positive sign of societal change across the globe when microfinance no longer needs to target and promote specific genders, races, or other demographics at the exclusion of others. The final case of caste embeddedness in India illustrates just how wide a gap remains for that to happen.

The second section focused on the role the Prosperity Gospel has played in shifting traditional African religious power dynamics and perceptions of wealth and the accumulation of wealth. While one might find fault in the Prosperity Gospel's contention that a greater level of faith in God will lead to both spiritual and material abundance on earth, it is difficult not to see the appeal of capitalism-based Christian movements that are rapidly sweeping poverty-stricken landscapes. However, the ultimate price that many African societies are paying by the injection of a hyper-version of Protestant individualism is the loss of traditional African cultural and religious leadership at a time when it is most needed to strengthen communities and to combat corruption. Of course, the main question is whether or not that so-called traditional African leadership has been up to those tasks and if movements like the Prosperity Gospel have simply come to fill a void caused by the lack of committed and effective leadership that seeks to benefit both rich and poor. Perhaps the most effective leaders who can be supported through microfinance and other development efforts are those that stand outside ineffective government channels and who are committed to helping everyone in the community, regardless of social status or religious belief.

The final section presented an in-depth case study of the religious foundations in Iran known as the *bonyads*. These foundations have the potential to transform the lives of the poor on a grand scale, but instead have become enormous slush funds that have lined the pockets of an invisible minority. These mysterious institutions represent an extreme along the spectrum of faith-based economic development in terms of transparency. By examining the destructive and wasteful excesses caused by a lack of proper oversight of the *bonyads*, the case study seeks to raise awareness that development organizations, especially faith-based ones, require that oversight and transparency to ensure that the mission of alleviating poverty is not lost. So often churches and other faith-based organizations receive a pass on their development activities from regulators and public scrutiny, with the implicit assumption that internal forces will keep them on their path of nobility. Sadly, history has proven over and over again that the less oversight an organization or individual receives, whether religious or political, the more likely it is to stray from a path of goodness.

5
Usury

"Profitless usurer, why dost thou use
So great a sum of sums, yet canst not live?"
William Shakespeare (Sonnet 4)

The chief complaint levied against microfinance is that its money-lending operations are usurious. Money lending in general has never quite escaped its pejorative label of usury, for which it has had a long history. In fact, when the ancient Roman politician Cato was asked what he thought of money lending he replied, "You might as well ask me what I think about murder."[1] Long before the Romans, Hindu manuscripts dating from 1500 BCE contain the earliest mention of usury in either religious or secular texts. Two separate admonitions are contained in a list of laws promulgated by the sage Manu to help recreate civilization after the great floods some 10,000 years ago. One admonition is included in a list of offences which also consist of defiling a damsel, breaking a vow, and selling one's wife or child.[2] The other is more descriptive:

> In money transactions interest paid at one time (not by install-ments) shall never exceed the double (of the principle); on grain, fruit, wool or hair, (and) beasts of burden it must not be more

---

[1] Marcus Tullius Cicero, *On the Good Life* (Penguin Classics. Harmondsworth: Penguin, 1971), 171.
[2] Manusmriti, *The Laws of Manu*, trans. G. Buhler (Oxford, UK: Clarendon Press, 1886), 73.

than five times (the original amount). Stipulated interest beyond the legal rate, being against (the law), cannot be recovered; they call that a usurious way (of lending); (the lender) is (in no case) entitled to (more than) give in the hundred; Let him not take interest beyond the year, nor such as is unapproved, nor compound interest, periodical interest, stipulated interest, and corporal interest.[3]

While usury is forbidden, the text makes clear that some interest within the legal rate was permissible. In another passage, the text cites a lawgiver named Vasishtha, who established a rule that an eightieth part of a hundred could be charged per month (1.25 percent or 15 percent per annum).[4] Later in the text, the two highest castes of Brahmin and Kshatriya, the priest and ruling classes respectively, are denied the ability to lend money at interest—unless in times of distress where they are permitted to lend to "a very sinful man at a small interest."[5] Presumably, this prevented exploitation of the lower castes by charging interest on a loan. By the second century CE the upper caste prohibition disappeared and no further religious restrictions prevented societies on the Indian subcontinent from quickly progressing to interest rate rules resembling those observed today.

The Abrahamic faith traditions (Judaism, Christianity, and Islam) took initial strides to prevent adherents from charging any interest on loans, grounding their arguments in scripture.[6] The following sections will trace the somewhat longer historical Jewish and Christian debates on usury and how these religious traditions have both evolved to draw distinctions between acceptable interest and usury. The section on Islam will take a deeper look at its stance on charging interest and show ways organizations have designed products

---

[3] Manusmriti, *The Laws of Manu*, 48.
[4] Manusmriti, *The Laws of Manu*, 48.
[5] Manusmriti, *The Laws of Manu*, 70.
[6] Hinduism and Buddhism address issues of avarice surrounding money lending, but they identify "usury" as lending money at exorbitant rates. Because microfinance lending does not conflict with Hindu or Buddhist beliefs or practices, a historical discussion on the topic is unnecessary for the purposes of this book. See: Wayne A. M. Visser and Alistair McIntosh, "A Short Review of the Historical Critique of Usury," in *Accounting, Business & Financial History*, vol. 8, no. 2 (London: Routledge, July 1998), 175–189.

specifically tailored to the needs of Muslim clients. Because Islam still explicitly forbids charging any interest on loans, the risk-sharing aspects of some of these loan products provide excellent examples for microfinance institutions wishing to incorporate these ideas into their own products.

Judaism

The book of Deuteronomy in the Hebrew Scriptures is explicit in its condemnation of charging interest:

> Do not charge your brother interest, whether on money or food or anything else that may earn interest. You may charge a foreigner interest, but not a brother Israelite, so that the LORD your God may bless you in everything you put your hand to in the land you are entering to possess.[7]

The books of Exodus (22:25) and Leviticus (25:35–37) contain admonitions against lending at interest that religious moneylenders have been able to circumvent through interpretation, but the passages in Deuteronomy (23:19–20) categorically state that Jews are not permitted to charge interest to one another. However, it *does* explicitly condone generating a profit on money lending with Gentiles. This is because Gentiles are not part of the Israelite brotherhood that suffered together in Egypt before making the arduous journey back to the Promised Land.[8] Later Christian reformers like Calvin drew upon this important distinction between Jews and Gentiles to support their arguments on usury, which will be discussed in the next section on Christianity. The biblical scholar Benjamin Nelson also reminds us that some have interpreted the verses in Deuteronomy as God allowing the Hebrews to take usury from alien peoples to indicate his wrath for Gentiles.[9]

Modern language separates usury and interest, but according to biblical scholar Susan Buckley, this is a recent construction. While

---

[7] Deuteronomy 23:19–20 (New International Version)

[8] Paul Johnson, *A History of the Jews* (London: Orion Books Ltd, 1987), 173.

[9] Benjamin Nelson, *The Idea of Usury: From Tribal Brotherhood to Universal Otherhood* (Chicago: University of Chicago Press, 1969), 54–55.

today we view usury as a rate of interest greater than that which the law or public opinion permits, Judaism has always equated the two in both scripture and practice.[10] A modern-day Jewish legal practice known as *heter 'iska* (meaning "permission of business partnership") is a religiously approved way of restructuring a loan so that the debt becomes an investment and the investor assumes some level of risk should the venture fail. These arrangements take the form of silent partnerships rather than joint ventures and the principal is due even in the case of business failure. These types of contracts are limited in scope to business ventures and are not necessarily suited to consumption loans, though some clever financiers have been successful in arguing that such things as mortgages should be included since they are indeed investments.[11] The complexities of these contracts make it difficult to resolve legal disputes (which are common in *heter 'iska*), particularly when the cases are brought into secular courtrooms.[12]

Some organizations have used the prohibition of interest as an inspiration to create interest-free loan programs to serve the poor. The International Association of Hebrew Free Loans and its forty-nine affiliate organizations throughout North America and other parts of the world have been providing interest-free loans for over a hundred years, primarily for economic assistance to recent Jewish immigrants.[13] The Hebrew Free Loan societies trace their roots to Eastern Europe, where for centuries similar associations helped to channel individual charitable contributions to support and sustain these funds. These groups brought this model with them to wherever they immigrated. The first of these, the Hebrew Free Loan Society of New York, was founded in 1892, grounding its work in the passages of Exodus and Leviticus mentioned previously and the Jewish tradition of *Gemilut Chassadim* (performing deeds of loving kindness). The society in New York also takes its inspiration from Maimonides's

---

[10] Susan L. Buckley, *Teachings on Usury in Judaism, Christianity and Islam* (Lewiston, New York: The Edwin Mellen Press, 2000), 1–2.

[11] Rabbi Meir Orlian, "What is a Heter Iska and How Does it Work," *Jewish Press*, 13 May 2009, http://www.businesshalacha.com/articles/heter-iska-101-ipes (accessed 4 January 2014).

[12] Kenneth H. Ryesky, "Secular Law Enforcement of the Heter 'Iska," JLaw.com, http://www.jlaw.com/Articles/heter1.html (accessed 4 January 2014).

[13] International Association of Jewish Free Loans, "About IAJFL," http://www.freeloan.org/about-iajfl/ (accessed 4 January 2014).

highest level of giving, and the history section on its website begins with this quote from the medieval thinker, "A loan is better than charity, for it enables one to help oneself." The New York society alone has provided over USD $200m in loans to 860,000 borrowers since its inception.[14] Pure interest-free lending requires a sustained donor base, and the Hebrew Free Loan societies have accomplished this through their shared faith and cultural connections.

Christianity

Although scripture made it clear to Jews whom they could charge interest to and whom they could not, early Christians were in an ambiguous position. In Buckley's words, "The teaching in the New Testament scriptures on usurious lending is couched in more ideal-istic and universalistic terms in the light of loving not only one's friends, but equally one's enemy and neighbor."[15] Nevertheless, many of the early church fathers co-opted the Deuteronomy position and applied it to Christians. Others like St. Thomas Aquinas turned to Aristotle to support their low opinion of lending at interest.[16]

The early and medieval Catholic Church quarreled over usury laws and whether or not they should prohibit Christians from lend-ing money at interest. At stake was whether Christians themselves were meant to be the "alien other" or part of a universal *brother-hood* that included the Israelites.[17] Many Christians at that time contended that usury was antithetical to the spirit of a brotherhood of all human beings.[18] This led to a gradual rise in Jewish lend-ing to Christians that firmly established Jews as the leading bank-ers in the early Middle Ages. However, Catholic clergy seeking to finance the Crusades and other "religious" activities opted for looser

---

[14] Hebrew Free Loan Society, "History," http://www.hfls.org/about-us/history (accessed 4 January 2014).

[15] Buckley, *Teachings on Usury*, 95.

[16] See *Summa Theologica*, IIa-IIae Q. 78. Aquinas restates Aristotle's position from the *Politics* (1258b1, trans. B. Jowett) that gaining money out of money is the most hated sort of wealth getting because money was intended to be used in exchange, but not to increase at interest. Interest is the birth of money from money, and this *of* money is unnatural.

[17] Nelson, *The Idea of Usury*, 8.

[18] Nelson, *The Idea of Usury*, 26.

interpretations of scripture in order to reverse usury laws to their advantage. Pope Leo X cut short the internal Catholic debate over usury by pronouncing the legitimacy of the five percent interest clause at the Fifth Lateran Council in 1515.[19]

Both Luther and Calvin came to recognize the benefits of charging interest on loans. However, Luther initially denounced usury as a diabolical invention that the Roman Catholic Church created to extort money from Germany.[20] In a 1520 sermon, he declared, "Charging for a loan is contrary to natural law."[21] Luther grounded his argument in the New Testament passage Luke 6:35, where Christ admonished his followers to lend without expecting anything in return.[22] It is not entirely clear from the passage, though, whether Christ was making an argument for the treatment of one's enemies or instantiating a universal value that should be applied to everyone. One interesting note is that the German word for debt (*Schuld*) is also the same word for guilt. This is perhaps an interesting reflection of the Protestant Ethic and its influence on German language and culture.

Nevertheless, Luther's virulent hatred against interest abated as he relented to the demands of the German nobility who relied heavily on interest-bearing loans to maintain the economy. Six years later, he wrote a letter to the prince of Saxony stating, "Interest which does not exceed four or five percent is not necessarily unjust."[23] He clarifies his new position in another letter to the same prince:

> Indeed it would be both tolerable and desirable that all other payments should be abolished, and a fifth or a sixth were collected from the people, as was done by Joseph in Egypt, but since there is no such orderly arrangement in the world, I must despair of this remedy and say that it is highly necessary that the taking of interest should be regulated everywhere, but to abolish it entirely would not be right either, for it can be made just.[24]

---

[19] Nelson, *The Idea of Usury*, 25.

[20] Nelson, *The Idea of Usury*, 32.

[21] Martin Luther, *Luther's Works*, Volume 45, ed. Jaroslav Pelikan (St. Louis, MO: Concordia Publishing House, 1955), 20.

[22] "But love your enemies, and do good, and lend, expecting nothing in return; and your reward will be great, and you will be sons of the Most High; for he is kind to the ungrateful and the selfish" (Revised Standard Version).

[23] Nelson, *The Idea of Usury*, 49.

[24] Nelson, *The Idea of Usury*, 52.

Luther's abrupt reversal points towards his increased awareness that loaning money at interest is necessary for a healthy economy and that the ideal natural world does not always match up with the real world. Calvin took a more literal interpretation of the passages in Deuteronomy, declaring them directed solely at Jews. He argued that the precept to lend without usury was plainly a part of the Jewish polity and not a universal "spiritual law." Otherwise, God would not have allowed the Hebrews to lend at usury to Gentiles.[25]

It is important to note that during this time the Christian struggle over usury generated hostility towards Jewish banking enterprises in Europe. Some prominent Jewish thinkers came to the defense of charging interest, proposing arguments that helped to address religious concerns over interest. The most compelling arguments came from Abraham Farissol, a sixteenth-century scribe living in Ferrara, Italy. He first attacked the Christian natural law argument against usury by appealing to Hebrew Scriptures. Farissol contended that after the original natural order of society was destroyed, a new order, different from the first, had been created—based on private property and profits. Except in the case of charity, society functioned with a price system that provided rent on property, wages, and fees for other borrowed things. To revert to the natural order of communal ownership and the free distribution of services would provoke discord. Thus, both religious and secular authorities have established the custom of asking a fair and agreed upon price for goods and services.[26] Farissol knew as well as the clergy that the concept of a natural society was a theoretical construct having no relationship to economic reality.

Farissol asked that if, in fact, the price system functioned in all markets of goods and services, should it not function as well in the money market? Was it not reasonable to expect a price for the use of money in the same manner as one expects a price for the use of non-fungible goods? Incidentally, his argument represents the modern definition of interest as the price for the use of one's money, and he added that the loan of this money is often more valuable to the borrower than a loan of a specific good.[27] Farissol reinforced his

---

[25] Nelson, *The Idea of Usury*, 75–76 (from Calvin's *Christian Restitutio LVI*).
[26] David B. Ruderman, *The World of the Renaissance Jew: The Life and Thought of Abraham Ben Mordecai Farissol* (Cincinnati: Hebrew Union College Press, 1981), 91.
[27] Ruderman, *The World of the Renaissance Jew*, 92.

argument by pointing out that the Fifth Lateran Council granted Christians the right to charge five percent interest on loans. He cited two other papal exceptions to the usury prohibition: those of interest on purchased rents and on dowries.[28] By also appealing to just-price theory, he hoped to transfer charging interest on loans to solid economic ground. According to Farissol, the alternative to borrowing money at interest was to buy on credit at a high price or to barter for other goods. Either way, one stood to lose more than by paying interest at an agreed upon rate.[29]

Most Christians and Jews have come to accept the modern-day separation between usury and interest, the former defined as an exorbitant rate of interest and the latter being woven into the fabric of economic life. For them, the debate has evolved into the issue of how to incorporate low-cost credit and debt finance into the structure of poverty-stricken communities.[30] Nevertheless, there are still voices within Christian communities that deride all forms of interest as usury, as evidenced by the following poem written by Peter Maurin, who co-founded the Catholic Worker Movement in 1933:

Banker - 1600 A.D.

1. Before John Calvin
   people were not allowed
   to lend money at interest.

2. John Calvin decided
   to legalize
   money-lending at interest
   in spite of the teachings
   of the Prophets of Israel
   and the Fathers of the Church.

3. Protestant countries
   tried to keep up with John Calvin
   and money-lending at interest
   became the general practice.

---

[28] Ruderman· *The World of the Renaissance Jew,* 93.
[29] Ruderman, *The World of the Renaissance Jew,* 96.
[30] Buckley, *Teachings on Usury,* 174.

4. And money ceased to be
a means of exchange
and began to be
a means to make money.

5. So people lent money on time
and started to think of time
in terms of money
and said to each other:
"Time is money."[31]

Neither the Catholic Worker nor Christian-based organizations provide interest-free loans on a scale even remotely close to the Hebrew Loan societies. Nevertheless, many Christian groups have become convinced of the benefits microfinance brings to communities and either actively promote or engage in microfinance efforts. In a rare statement signed by the Evangelical Lutheran Church of America in 1999, leaders in the church explicitly call for "funding of micro-enterprises and other community development projects that can empower low-income people economically."[32] Support from Christian leaders represents a healthy progression away from the usurious debate and towards productive remedies for the poor.

"Fair" interest rates in microfinance

Many people new to microfinance are shocked when learning about the interest rates charged and how drastically they differ from the interest rates they might be paying on their own outstanding debts (e.g. the average interest rate on microfinance loans in India is twenty six percent which is on the lower end

---

[31] The Catholic Worker Movement, "A Collection of Peter Maurin's Essays," http://www.catholicworker.org/roundtable/easyessays.cfm#<STRONG>Banker – 1600 A.D.</STRONG> (accessed 4 January 2014).
[32] Evangelical Lutheran Church of America, "A Social Statement on: Sufficient, Sustainable Livelihood for All," Adopted by a more than two-thirds majority vote by the sixth Churchwide Assembly of the Evangelical Lutheran Church in America, meeting in Denver, Colorado, 16–22 August 1999. http://download.elca.org/ELCA%20Resource%20Repository/Economic_LifeSS.pdf (accessed 4 January 2014).

of the global average of thirty five percent[33] given government-mandated interest rate caps, which often result in less rural outreach due to higher costs). The short answer to the question of why they are so "high" (high being a relative term) is that in many cases the interest rate is set such that it can support the costly work of the microfinance institution. Traditional banks have long known these costs and thus shy away from engaging in transactions under specific dollar amounts. It is very challenging to service a $120 loan made to a person living in a remote area, not just in terms of disbursing funds, but the consistent repayments and follow-up needed to recover the loan. Multiply that by thousands of people that an institution serves, often in areas with poor infrastructure, and costs rise dramatically.

One main difference between microfinance loans and those offered by loan sharks is compounding, which can have a drastic effect on the overall price of a loan. For example, a loan of $120 offered by a microfinance lender at a 3% flat monthly interest rate for twelve months means that each month the client will pay back $10 in principal and $3.60 in interest, for a grand total of $120 in principal repayments and $43.20 in interest by the end of the one year term (using the simple interest formula). The effective interest rate on this loan is 81%. If the microfinance lender shifts from flat interest rates to the declining balance method (paying interest only on the amount outstanding), the total interest payments amount to only $23.40 and the effective interest rate drops to 42.5% (assuming equal payments). A major trend in microfinance has been to put pressure on lenders to shift to the declining balance method for calculating interest since it is both fair to the client and incentivizes them to pay loans off as quickly as they can.

Now, if the same client took out a $120 loan with a loan shark quoting 2% interest (presumably more attractive to an unsuspecting client comparing prices based solely on quoted interest rates), but compounded and paid weekly for a year, he or she would be paying $124.80 in interest payments on the loan, for a whopping effective interest rate of 400%.

---

[33] Christoph Kneiding and Richard Rosenberg, "Variations in Microcredit Interest Rates," CGAP.org, 1 July 2008, http://www.cgap.org/publications/variations-microcredit-interest-rates (accessed 4 January 2014).

Another trend in microfinance has been to ensure transparency in prices charged to clients by revealing the Annual Percentage Rate (APR) on each loan offered to clients to show the true cost of borrowing money from the lender. While low monthly interest rates attract clients, things like upfront fees, compulsory deposits, insurance, taxes, and the calculation method can significantly increase the cost of a loan. Chuck Waterfield from MF Transparency has made great strides in raising awareness in the industry around this (Please visit MF Transparency's website for more information: http://www.mftransparency.org/).

Islam

While the Judeo-Christian debate over usury has resulted in widespread abandonment of the image of the natural world for just-price economics, Islam has yet to be convinced of this. The Qur'an explicitly forbids usury, or *riba*[34], in four different revelations. Three of the revelations express misgivings over *riba*, while the fourth severely censures those who engage in it:

> Those that live on usury (*riba*) shall rise up before God like men whom Satan has demented by his touch; for they claim that trading is no different from usury. But God has permitted trading and made usury unlawful. He that has received an admonition from his Lord and mended his ways may keep his previous gains; God will be his judge. Those that turn back shall be the inmates of the Fire, wherein they shall abide forever. God has laid His curse on usury and blessed alms-giving (*zakat*) with increase. God bears no love for the impious and the sinful. Those that have faith and do good works, attend to their prayers and render the alms levy, will be rewarded by their Lord and will have nothing to fear or to regret. Believers have fear of God and waive what is still due to you from usury, if your faith be true; or war shall be declared against your God and His apostle. If you repent you may retain your principal, suffering no loss and causing loss to none. If your debtor be in straits, grant him a delay until he can discharge his

---

[34] The word "riba" is derived from the root r.b.w., meaning to grow, increase, or augment. Interestingly, the word for interest in Hebrew is "ribbit."

debt; but if you waive the sum as alms it will be better for you, if you but knew it. (Surah Al-Basqarah ii.275–280)[35]

While the Hebrew Scriptures simply forbid usury,[36] the above passage from the Qur'an assures Muslims that God will cast the unrepentant usurious person into the flames of hell for eternity. Despite its own historical debate on what *riba* actually means, Islam has not relented to pressures from the marketplace and has continued to maintain its stance that charging interest on loans is usurious and a violation of Islamic law.[37] The logic behind this is simple. Lending money at interest without any means of sharing risk between lender and borrower creates a relationship where weak and vulnerable individuals can be easily exploited by more powerful ones. This explains why contracts used in Islamic finance are generally a page or two in length—they need to be clear enough to all signatories and contain no loopholes that might benefit one party over another in a way that is not obvious.

By differentiating trade from usury, the Qur'an reaffirms the practice of trading as a respectable profession. After all, Muhammad and his early followers were traders. The importance of trading partnerships in Islam has stimulated financial intermediaries to find creative ways to help Muslims access loans without violating Islamic law. When microfinance institutions first introduced lending models into predominantly Muslim communities, they met with harsh critics who labeled their practices as violations of Islamic law. Their challenge was how to structure the loans in a way that would conform to Islamic law and eliminate *riba*. Each product is considered Sharia compliant, meaning that it conforms to Sharia (Islamic) law[38] and

---

[35] N. J. Dadwood, *The Koran* (London: Penguin Books, 1990), 286.

[36] Deuteronomy 23:19 20 ("Do not charge your brother interest, whether on money or food or anything else that may earn interest. You may charge a foreigner interest, but not a brother Israelite, so that the LORD your God may bless you in everything you put your hand to in the land you are entering to possess.").

[37] Buckley, *Teachings on Usury*, 192.

[38] Sharia law is based on interpretations of the holy book of Islam, the Qur'an, and a collection of stories recounted about the prophet Muhammad and his early followers, called the *Sunnah* or the *Hadith*. Islamic jurists analyze these two primary sources to address legal questions and issues. For modern questions, much of this boils down to asking "what would Muhammad

not considered unlawful or forbidden (*haram*).[39] The following sections illustrate a few examples where organizations have integrated some of these methods into their microfinance work with Muslim communities.

Murabaha (reselling an asset)

Save the Children, a Christian development organization, ran a credit-based project for Bani Hamida farmers in Jordan by developing a strict lending system established on the principles of *murabaha*. The project leaders found themselves stuck between headquarters who refused to support an interest-free loan project, and the Bani Hamida farmers who felt they were being pressed by a western organization to go against their religion if they used the original product. Rather than loaning the money directly to borrowers, Save the Children purchased the goods (or animals) for them. The borrower then repaid the purchase price of the goods plus a six percent service fee, not interest, charge. One advantage to *murabaha* is that it ensures that loans are spent on what they were originally intended, and by using it, Save the Children was able to make loans to farmers to build fences around orchards and construct water tanks to irrigate them.[40]

While *murabaha* is the most prevalent Sharia compliant product offered by microfinance institutions, it contains many flaws. First, it places the burden on the lenders to purchase goods, making it a cumbersome operation requiring a great deal of coordination and expertise. It also makes the lenders vulnerable to collusion between borrowers and sellers of goods in the marketplace. From a social performance perspective its primary shortcoming comes from the lack of input on pricing from the borrower. While price negotiations are not entirely normal in standard microfinance contracts, shifting to a Sharia model should represent an entire shift in culture

---

and/or his early followers have done in a given situation?" In cases where the Qur'an and Sunnah cannot help, jurists are permitted to render legal opinions, or *fatwa*, based on their own informed reasoning. This makes Islamic law both a rich environment for scholarly discourse and a fertile ground for potential controversy. The word "Sharia" in Arabic means "way" or "path to a water source".

[39] *Haram* literally means "sinful" and is used to classify acts that are forbidden by Muslims as they are considered *hated* by God.

[40] Buckley, *Teachings on Usury*, 272.

and thinking. *Murabaha* conforms to the letter of Sharia law, but a *musawama* (see Box below) contract that involves a mutually derived upon price between the borrower and the microfinance institution might go further in capturing the true spirit of trading sought after in the law. Of course, by including the borrower's voice into the transaction, this would require an extra step that might complicate the contract process.

Musharaka (joint venture)

In traditional *musharaka*, the borrower provides part of the capital needed (usually about thirty percent) and is responsible for managing the project or business. The microfinance institution provides the remaining capital, supervision, and technical assistance. At the end of the project, the borrower receives about two-thirds of the profits and the remaining third is split between the borrower and the microfinance institution, based on the amount of money each contributed.[41] This type of system encourages the institution and any technical partners it has to provide the client with supervision and assistance because the institution now has a stake in the success of the venture.

Very few microfinance institutions have taken steps to introduce *musharaka* into their products. However, one organization operating in the far eastern province of Manipur, India in the remote mountainous area near Myanmar has implemented "business share loan" products based on *musharaka*. CAPARV, the Council for Anti Poverty Action and Rural Volunteers, was established in the city of Imphal in 1988 to focus on economic development, conflict resolution, forest rights, and HIV/AIDS. The organization has no official religious ties, but its entire management staff and about half of its clients are Muslims. The following describes how CAPARV employs a "business share loan" to a female Muslim client:

> The CAPARV fieldworker shows her how to keep a simple record of sales and stocks, and the records are checked once a week by the fieldworker. The surplus made on sales of goods which the borrower has bought with her loan are quite easily calculated,

---

[41] Buckley, *Teachings on Usury,* 272–273.

and CAPARV is entitled to one-quarter of the total for the period of the loan, usually one year. If the goods do not sell, or have to be sold at a loss, the woman only has to repay the principal, with no extra charges.[42]

Microfinance researcher and practitioner Malcolm Harper affirms that by using this system, CAPARV has been able to cover its costs and satisfy its Muslim clients. This system requires a great deal of trust on both sides, and so far there has been no evidence of falsified figures by clients or fieldworkers. CAPARV is widely known and respected in the community, and according to Harper, the clients "are very aware that these loans have a certain religious significance, because the system has been especially designed to conform to Sharia principles."[43]

Mudaraba (limited liability partnership)

Unlike in *musharaka*, where all the partners can participate in the management of the business and can work for it, *mudaraba* does not allow for investor involvement. The Grameen Bank uses a system that somewhat resembles *mudaraba* limited liability partnerships, but does not ask its borrowers to share in the profits with lenders. How can they loan money at interest in Muslim communities without violating Islamic law? Because each borrower is also an owner in the bank, Grameen argues that borrowers in effect pay interest to the companies they own, and therefore to themselves.[44] According to Yunus, Muslim communities do not initially recognize the subtle difference in banking techniques and are quick to condemn his efforts. Grameen trains its bank workers to overcome opposition from political and religious leaders without endangering their own safety and that of the women they serve. Gradually, people come to accept them once they understand the ownership

---

[42] Malcolm Harper, D. S. K. Rao, and Ashis Kumar Sahu, *Development, Divinity and Dharma: The role of Religion in Development and Microfinance Institutions* (Rugby, Warwickshire, UK: Practical Action Publishing, 2008), 130.

[43] Harper et al., *Development, Divinity and Dharma*, 131.

[44] When the Grameen Bank accepted the Nobel Peace Prize in 2006, the Nobel Committee asked for the entire bank to come to Norway to accept the prize. For that, Muhammad Yunus responded by clarifying that the bank was made up of six million members.

structure and the benefits it brings to others. Opposition eventually dies off, but they often have to repeat the same battle in every new village.[45]

Qard Hassan (free loans)

In addition to interest-free loans using alternative Sharia compliant methods, some microfinance institutions have begun offering entirely free loans to Muslim communities with support from *zakat* contributions. One of the five pillars of Islam, *zakat*, is the requirement of all practicing Muslims to contribute 2.5 percent of annual wealth (not income) towards specific social causes such as helping the extreme poor with the ultimate aim of helping to lift them out of poverty. This practice has remained a cornerstone of economic development for centuries and in the modern era has been institutionalized by some governments. For example, as part of a broader Islamization of Pakistan, the government introduced the welfare system in 1980 through a law known as the *Zakat and Ushr Ordinance*.[46] This new law made *zakat* contributions compulsory nationwide through an annual tax collected within the financial system.

At least one microfinance institution in Pakistan, named Asasah and discussed in the next chapter, has begun offering *Qard Hassan* (free loans) to the extreme poor in that country. Perhaps in the future, willing donors could channel their annual *zakat* contributions to organizations like Asasah instead of through government-controlled channels (which may lack full accountability). This could offer an excellent way to infuse an established tenet of almsgiving with the principles of helping the poor help themselves, all in a way that captures the spirit of Sharia law.

---

[45] Muhammad Yunus, *Banker to the Poor* (New York: Public Affairs, 2003), 110.

[46] See https://www.google.com/url?sa=t&rct=j&q=&esrc=s&source=web&cd=3&cad=rja&ved=0CEEQFjAC&url=http%3A%2F%2Fpunjablaws.punjab.gov.pk%2Findex%2Fgetaspdf%2Fref%2Fd0c499f0-7096-4ab4-bdfd-c5f6eb9ad6e7&ei=Xo6GUZOkEovC9QTN7oC4Bg&usg=AFQjCNHCaHbd48oWl8I3004R8PGojxIxfQ&sig2=GvDJ4-rF1wwW_yhcnSXPsQ&bvm=bv.45960087,d.eWU (accessed 4 January 2014).

List of Sharia compliant products used in microfinance[47]

1. *Ijara:* Asset-based financing through leasing with a second
   contract to purchase the asset(s) at the end of a lease period.
   This is not widely used in microfinance as it is normally used
   in retail finance for consumption purposes such as home
   mortgages, cars, and other household needs that are often not
   offered by microfinance institutions. Currently used to a small
   degree in Yemen, where the government regulator has listed it
   among approved Sharia products.
2. *Joala*: Payment of upfront fees. While this product often quali-
   fies under Sharia rules, it goes the least in capturing the spirit
   of Sharia law in that it does not share risk and does little to
   protect vulnerable individuals from exploitation. Widely used
   in Iraq and other areas where it is allowed.
3. *Mudaraba:* A limited liability partnership that generally
   does not allow for direct investor involvement. This is not
   widely used in microfinance as it requires matching investors
   and clients, with the microfinance institution acting as the
   intermediary.
4. *Murabaha:* Asset-based financing through purchasing goods
   for borrowers and reselling it to them at a mark-up. This is the
   most widely used method in microfinance, primarily because
   it most resembles the trading practices of early Muslims.
5. *Musawama:* The microfinance institution and borrower arrive
   at an agreed upon price for an asset. This is similar to *murabaha*, but involves some form of bargaining between the institution and the borrower rather than a set price. Not as widely
   used in microfinance as *murabaha*.
6. *Musharaka:* A joint venture with profit and loss sharing. Not
   widely used for similar reasons cited in *mudaraba*. However, there

---

[47] This list is not exhaustive since it continues to grow as microfinance institutions develop ways to incorporate traditional Islamic financial instruments
in their work. To gain a greater understanding of Islamic finance, the reader
might want to pick up a copy of Ibrahim Warde's definitive book on the
field entitled *Islamic Finance in the Global Economy* (Edinburgh: Edinburgh
University Press, 2010).

is massive growth potential here as some microfinance institutions have began developing products where the institution itself becomes the investor and assists borrowers with their businesses.

7. **Qard Hassan:** Interest-free loans with no other fees attached, usually to students or the very poor. Some microfinance institutions have begun offering this product as a means to channel targeted grant funding such as compulsory almsgiving (*zakat*) stipulated as an annual 2.5 percent of total wealth that must be given to the poor by all Muslims.

8. **Salam:** An advanced purchase of an asset by the microfinance institution and delivered on a future date set by the borrower. This is commonly used in agricultural financing, where the commodities being sold are not in existence at the time of the sale.

Navigating Muslim religion and culture

The story of the Alfalah Development Institute illustrates the religious and cultural challenges non-Muslim faith-based organizations face when working in Muslim communities. Alfalah was formed in 1986 by church leaders, business people, and professionals as a Christian development organization to address poverty concerns in Pakistan. It specialized in micro-enterprise development by providing people with access to credit and livelihood training. In an interview for the *Christian Action Journal*, Bishop Nazir-Ali, one of its founders, articulated the difficulties the Christian NGO faced while working in a predominately Muslim country:

Islamic fundamentalists oppose Alfalah for they see it as a threat even though Alfalah makes loans to both Muslims and Christians ... The question of interest hangs like a sword, because charging interest in Pakistan is illegal. We offer loans attached to which is a service charge to help with the administration and training costs of Alfalah, but any Christian NGO involved in this work lays itself open to the accusation of usury. However, we retain good relations with large sections of Muslim society. Our banking and legal advisors are Muslims. Loans are made to Muslims as well as Christians.[48]

---

[48] From an interview with Bishop Michael Nazir-Ali in St. Anselm's Church Hall, Kennington Cross, London: "Opportunity," *Christian Action Journal*, Autumn 1993, 12–13 (quoted in Buckley, *Teachings on Usury*, 275).

This interview illuminates how important it is for development organizations, especially faith-based ones, to be aware of possible religious and cultural concerns about money lending. While debates over usury, especially in Muslim communities, continue to be a lightning rod for criticism, they often serve as masks to hide deeper theological issues.

Some of the examples in this section reveal a strong tension between traditional Islamic values and western values that has overshadowed the usury debate. Many Muslims react negatively not only to the possibility of violating Islamic usury laws, but also to what they perceive as pressure from the West to conform to its values. As we have seen, some organizations like Grameen have structured their operations to align with Sharia law by making client members owners in the bank. They have also spent time educating borrowers and religious leaders about the benefits that microfinance offers the community. Similarly, Save the Children won the support and approval of Jordanian farmers by developing financial assistance in specific Islamic terms to ensure that clients do not compromise their religious values or feel threatened by western influence.[49]

Banking based on the principles of sharing profits and losses and risk in general fulfills the Qur'anic requirements on *riba* by introducing trade- and investment-oriented activities in place of credit activities, while eliminating interest from the banking system.[50] The major drawback to this system of banking is its cumbersome nature and the inefficiency of having to match all of the stakeholders together for some of the products. Nevertheless, it encourages a unified relationship of risk sharing between lenders and borrowers tragically absent from traditional financial instruments and investments. By looking beyond the religious and cultural motivations for these products and focusing on the universal respect for human relationships they cultivate, both microfinance and traditional bankers can recognize the immense value these products can deliver. Incorporating these types of risk-sharing methods into formal banking transactions carries the promise of strengthening various sectors of the market economy— and perhaps even social society itself.

---

[49] Buckley, *Teachings on Usury,* 274.
[50] Buckley, *Teachings on Usury,* 265–267.

6
Inspired Microfinance

"Remember, aid cannot achieve the end of poverty. Only homegrown development based on the dynamism of individuals and firms in free markets can do that."[1]

William Easterly

Proponents of microfinance see their work as creating a level playing field for everybody. Muhammad Yunus argues, "When we want to help the poor, we usually offer them charity. Most often, we use charity to avoid recognizing the problem and finding a solution for it. Charity becomes a way to shrug off our responsibility. But charity is no solution to poverty. Charity only perpetuates poverty by taking the initiative away from the poor."[2] Nevertheless, charity has its place in the world as a short-term stopgap measure, particularly when serving those living at the very base of the poverty pyramid whose primary needs cover food, shelter, and clothing. Perhaps some of them will eventually "graduate" beyond charity. But sadly, there may always be people who for whatever reason might never progress beyond charity. The risk of assuming otherwise potentially sets people up for catastrophe if we remove the last resort safety net that charity offers. The challenge for faith organizations is how they can

---

[1] William Easterly, *White Man's Burden: Why the West's Efforts to Aid the Rest Have Done So Much Ill and So Little Good* (New York: Penguin Books, 2006), 322.
[2] Muhammad Yunus, *Banker to the Poor* (New York: Public Affairs, 2003), 249.

branch out from charity and support microfinance as one of many solutions to the problems of poverty, while remaining true to their core competencies and principles.

At a time when organized religion has been under fire for contributing to the violence among people and nations, and in many ways standing in the way of an individual's connection to Spirit, it is not easy to make the case for faith-based economic development. Indeed, how far faith organizations should tread into economic ventures, community or otherwise, is a difficult question as it raises the issue of potential mission drift. This presents potential problems for all faith organizations that engage in microfinance, especially when juxtaposed against Weber's conclusion mentioned in Chapter 3 that the spirit of religious asceticism has left us bound in an iron cage of materialism.[3] Microfinance *can* lead to community development. However, it still represents a promotion of capitalistic principles, and faith communities need to be watchful of their own traditions and motivations to ensure that factors such as hyper-asceticism and self-reliance do not ultimately lead to damaging the communities they serve.

Convinced of the benefits microfinance brings to communities, many religious groups have begun either promoting or actively engaging in microfinance. As mentioned in Chapter 5, in a statement signed by the Evangelical Lutheran Church of America, leaders in the church explicitly call for the "funding of micro-enterprises and other community development projects that can empower low-income people economically."[4] Indeed, faith organizations can play an essential role in bringing a spiritual grounding to microfinance. Religious leaders are in a unique position to provide powerful advocacy to generous people wanting to form partnerships with poor communities. By working with microfinance institutions, religious groups can help protect the interests of the poorest of the poor and at the same time nourish the spiritual needs of their own congregations.

Microfinance is not a panacea to cure all ills that plague the poor. Nevertheless, it presents the poor with an opportunity to work

---

[3] Max Weber, *The Protestant Ethic and the Spirit of Capitalism* (Mineola, NY: Dover Publications, 2003), 182.
[4] Evangelical Lutheran Church of America (ELCA), "A Social Statement on: Sufficient, Sustainable Livelihood for All," adopted by a more than two-thirds majority vote by the sixth Churchwide Assembly of the Evangelical Lutheran Church in America, meeting in Denver, Colorado, 16–22 August 1999.

together to rise from poverty and create stronger communities. Partnerships between microfinance institutions and faith organizations have the potential to generate a powerhouse of economic influence resting on a solid moral foundation. It also gives people of faith an outlet for loving their neighbor not by falling into paternalistic relationships based on charity, but by offering genuine opportunities for people to transform their lives by becoming savers over the long term. Crucial for the success of savings programs is that people have confidence that their money will be safe, and faith organizations are in a unique position in that people trust them (as long as they do not violate that trust). This is not an entirely new relationship, since temples in Ancient Egypt were originally used for storing wealth. Indeed, for the sake of the poorest of the poor, God and Mammon *can* work together.

In fact, several major international economic development organizations have been established through some form of religious inspiration. One explanation is that many religious values of care for the poor and fellow human beings, whether neighbors or strangers, are rooted in universal principles which form the central focus of religious teachings. For many of these development organizations, the shedding of their religious roots has become a natural consequence of their evolution. But for others, religion remains a strong pillar within the organization and how it operates. The following sections will explore examples of organizations along this spectrum in order to illustrate cases where a symbiotic relationship between religion and economic development persists and others where the initial religious inspiration ignites a flame that no longer requires that continued connection.

Center for Community Transformation (Manila, Philippines)

An ongoing debate within the microfinance industry has left the question open of whether organizations should focus on financial products *only* or seek to address a wide range of products and services that each addresses a fundamental need of their clients. It is natural to assume the efficacy of taking a holistic approach to development, where credit, savings, and insurance make up only a portion of an organization's work alongside other things like livelihood training, health education, and community development projects.

Source: © 2014 Courtesy of Chris Dunford and Freedom from Hunger

However, development organizations frequently attract passionate people with big ideas, and trying to implement too many of them under a single umbrella can lead to a reduction in quality either by creating an expensive and wasteful bureaucracy if done on a large scale or paralysis through half-finished projects in the case of smaller organizations trying to do everything. Either the microfinance locomotive depicted in the above picture is not strong enough to pull its service cars or worse, it derails altogether. Specialization allows for maintaining a core competency in a single area and potentially doing it well. Overall client success can then come from developing strategic alliances with other players who provide the missing services.

One organization in the Philippines has been challenging the specialization argument in its work with the poor in metro Manila. The Center for Community Transformation (CCT) was founded in 1992 by Ms. Ruth Callanta with its mission: "As followers of Jesus Christ, we join the Holy Spirit in God's work of transforming lives

and communities."[5] In addition to microfinance, CCT has established the following program area units: Education, Health, Social
Security, Community Mobilization and Empowerment, Spiritual
Development, and the Kaibigan Ministry (a program to assist families formerly living on the street).[6] Through these program areas,
CCT strives to achieve its vision: "We hope to see Christ-centered
faith communities where Jesus Christ is honored and worshiped and
where people live with dignity and sufficiency in accordance with
God's plan for a just, humane, and caring society."[7]

CCT initially had difficulty integrating faith into their development
work. In the early years, they focused solely on training and consul-
tancy, winning a contract to help five thousand workers laid off from
the San Miguel brewery to start businesses of their own.[8] As Ms. Ruth
put it, CCT's "psychosocial-spiritual intervention would help them
see who they were in God's eyes, appreciate their worth as human
beings created in His image, and realize that this—their intrinsic
value–was not in any way contingent on their work in San Miguel."[9]
That led to another project through San Miguel to help a small community after the closing of one of its affiliate distilleries, where CCT
began doing microfinance.[10] The more financial success CCT achieved
in those first few years, the more Ms. Ruth saw the organization
becoming a "two headed hydra" that was losing its way. Interestingly,
she attributes this to hiring people of different faiths such as Muslims,
Mormons, and a Hare Krishna. As she put it, "I realized that, in an
organization that was founded primarily to share the Word of God—
founded on the premise that unless you accept the Lordship of Jesus
Christ, there can be no true transformation—you cannot have staff
colleagues of different faiths. In an organization that advocates for
one belief, you cannot have people having different faiths."[11]

---

[5] Center for Community Transformation, "Mission," http://cct.org.ph/about/
mission/ (accessed 4 January 2014).

[6] Center for Community Transformation, "Microfinance," http://cct.org.ph/
microfinance// (accessed 4 January 2014).

[7] Center for Community Transformation, "Vision," http://cct.org.ph/about/
vision/ (accessed 4 January 2014).

[8] Sylvia Palugod, *Toward the Abundant Life: Transforming Lives, Transforming
Communities* (Manila: OMF Literature, 2008), 29.

[9] Palugod, *Toward the Abundant Life,* 29.

[10] Palugod, *Toward the Abundant Life,* 33.

[11] Palugod, *Toward the Abundant Life,* 36–37.

After leaving CCT from1995 to 1998 (known as her years in the wilderness)[12], Ms. Ruth returned to a financially and spiritually struggling organization and committed herself to integrating faith and development into all of CCT's work. It had pastors on the staff who did not want to do microfinance, and the fifty percent repayment rate reflected a basic lack of understanding on how to manage a credit program.[13] After addressing the need for a cultural shift within the organization towards a more Christ-centered approach, the first change she made was to change their model away from the Grameen method over to one used by the Association for Social Advancement (ASA) in Bangladesh. Sometimes referred to as the Ford Motor Model of Microfinance, the ASA methodology seeks to standardize operations similar to an assembly line in order to reduce costs and ensure maximum efficiency. The main difference was the shedding of Grameen's group methodology in favor of the individual one offered by ASA. Ultimately, this fit better with CCT's objective of transforming lives by strengthening the relationship between both staff and client members with God, which they see as an individual process done in community with others. However, CCT's model triggers similar questions that Chapter 3 raised about the shift away from the "cumbersome" group lending model offered by Grameen and towards more efficiency through the individual lending model. However, CCT has mitigated some of this through incorporated fellowships where groups of 12–20 members meet each week at one of the member's residence to "study a portion of the Scriptures, pay their loans, make savings deposits, share successes, and pray for each others' business or personal problems."[14]

Over time as CCT attracted the attention of wealthy Christian donors, it established separate entities under the Foundation's umbrella, each focusing on different areas of development. The CCT Credit Cooperative was established in 2003, focused solely on microfinance and with offices in 23 provinces, 49 cities, and 42 towns of the Philippines.[15] Both the Spiritual Development program and the Community Mobilization and Empowerment program are designed to

---

[12] Palugod, *Toward the Abundant Life,* 45.
[13] Palugod, *Toward the Abundant Life,* 57.
[14] Center for Community Transformation, "Microfinance."
[15] Center for Community Transformation, "Microfinance."

train their client members to lead their communities by giving them training and support to develop themselves as leaders from spiritual, socio-political, cultural, and economic perspectives. The goal is to help the client member transform into a positive role model for their community to follow.[16] Ultimately, CCT has built on the success of forming strategic alliances with separate partners, primarily through the separate program entities within a single umbrella model. The next few sections outline some of the other program areas where CCT works.

Kaibigan Ministry

Named for the Filipino word for friend, CCT started the Kaibigan Ministry program in 2005 to help street dwellers living in an impoverished district of Manila. The program is divided up into four phases. The first phase involves CCT feeding, counseling, and holding Christian fellowship meetings with them. During the second phase, CCT finds them temporary shelter, along with access to social services such as medical care and educational assistance. During the third phase, CCT transitions people from street dwellers to long-term housing where they can participate in agriculture and food production. The fourth phase is reserved for those who want to learn additional livelihood or enterprise management skills, and CCT provides them with training and mentoring opportunities.[17]

Over time, participants in the fourth phase of the program grew to such an extent that with CCT's help they formed the Kaibigang Maaasahan Multi-Purpose Cooperative (KMMC)—the first cooperative in the Philippines with a membership composed of former street dwellers. The KMMC office is located at the Kaibigan Community Center in Pasay City (metro Manila), the hub from which CCT serves street dwellers. The center houses toilet, bath and laundry facilities, a preschool, clinic, a used clothing store, a water station (where they give out free filtered water to area residents), and a kitchen that makes affordable meals to the surrounding community. In addition to its location in metro Manila, CCT created a village four hours north of Manila where

---

[16] Center for Community Transformation, "Community Mobilization and Empowerment," http://cct.org.ph/community-mobilization-and-empower ment/ (accessed 4 January 2014).

[17] Center for Community Transformation, "Kaibigan Ministry," http://cct.org. ph/kaibigan-ministry/ (accessed 4 January 2014).

former street dwelling families can resettle and build a new life on a self-sustaining agricultural cooperative. Additionally, CCT has two boarding schools three hours south of Manila dedicated to educating children born on the streets.[18] Since the program's inception, CCT has helped thousands of former street dwellers turn their lives around.

Education

In addition to the two residential schools offered through their Kaibigan program, CCT manages thirty non-residential preschools in communities where it has microfinance operations. The pupils come from the poorest of the poor in those communities or are children of microfinance clients. They also help dropouts and underemployed adults obtain a high school education through their ten-month Alternative Learning System program. For those seeking technical experience, CCT established the CCT Training and Development Institute in 2006 that offers courses in electrical installation and maintenance, masonry, rough carpentry, and plumbing. Finally, the CCT Credit Cooperative offers higher education microfinance loans for those wanting to take the next step in their academic career but who cannot afford it.[19]

Social security and health

Established in 2000, the Visions of Hope Foundation is a separate entity under the CCT umbrella that began by providing cash assistance to support the primary and secondary education of abandoned, orphaned, and neglected children in urban and rural poor communities where the CCT Microfinance program operates. Through the Foundation, CCT provides the childhood education programs described above, access to life and health insurance, and also health services, which include the following:

- Free basic medical consultation at the twenty six clinics where CCT has a connection
- Health and environment lectures conducted by doctors once a month on topics such as leptospirosis, pulmonary tuberculosis, family planning, nutrition, diarrhea, urinary tract infection, first aid, climate change, personal and environmental hygiene,

---

[18] Center for Community Transformation, "Kaibigan Ministry."
[19] Center for Community Transformation, "Education."

pneumonia, malaria, dengue, cervical cancer, and how to treat the common cough, cold, and fever

- PTB-DOTS (Pulmonary Tuberculosis Bacilli-Directly Observed Treatment Short Course) program implemented in partnership with the Research Institute of Tuberculosis/Japan Anti-Tuberculosis Association and with local health centers.
- Feeding of malnourished children in partnership with Bethesda Ministries (bethesdacareinternational.org/)
- Family planning services in partnership with local NGOs
- Free flu vaccination
- Free basic dental care including oral health lectures for children and adults, oral prophylaxis, tooth extraction, fluoride treatment, and distribution of toothbrushes[20]

With devotional at the office each morning, corporate devotionals every Saturday, and ministers serving each branch (called Branch Pastors), CCT had made the internal transformation that enmeshed its work with Protestant Christianity. On the microfinance side, in addition to the Branch Pastor, Peer Servants (as opposed to the usual *Loan Officer* nomenclature) work with client members. On occasions when client members are late with their payment, both the Branch Pastor and Peer Servant travel to their home or place of business to pray with them for the money to come from God. These practices sprouting from an embedded Christian direction may strike some readers as crossing normative lines. Indeed, CCT is operating at the forefront of faith-based development in an environment where its selected client members are already part of Christian communities, so CCT views their role in furthering and deepening their transformation along both spiritual and economic lines. One thing to note is that the 2011 Religion & Public Life report put out by Pew Research ranked the Philippines as the country with the fifth-largest Christian Population (eighty seven million), with eighty two percent of Catholic and eleven percent of Protestant.[21] So, it is one of the

---

[20] Center for Community Transformation, "Health," http://cct.org.ph/health/ (accessed 4 January 2014).

[21] Pew Research Center, "Regional Distribution of Christians," 19 December 2011, http://www.pewforum.org/2011/12/19/global-christianity-regions/ (accessed 4 January 2014).

few countries in the world that can still refer to itself as a "Christian Nation"—barring the heavily concentrated Muslim population in the southern province of Mindanao. Thus, CCT's work must be viewed within this religious context. The author of CCT's organizational history unabashedly sums up CCT's development philosophy in the last sentence of her book, "Yes, there *is* an answer to poverty. His name is Jesus."[22]

Yayasan Sosial Bina Sejahtera (Cilacap, Indonesia)

In 1972, the Australian Oblates of Mary Immaculate (OMI), an arm of the Catholic Church, established a mission in the small town of Cilacap in southern Java to convert the locals to Christians. A year after the mission was opened, Father Charlie Burrows, an Irish missionary of the OMI, came to Cilacap. Born in Dublin, Fr. Charlie spent his adolescence working to help support his financially strapped family, maintaining a strong determination to become a priest. As he puts it, after graduating from seminary, he was "exported" to Australia over his modern and progressive views that went against conservative Catholic teaching.[23] After a few years in Australia, he was then "exiled" to the Indonesian jungle. His first tasks were helping to build schools and a Catholic hospital in town, but he quickly realized that in order to achieve its long-term objectives, the church would need its own fleet of trucks. These were instrumental in the early road and infrastructure build-out that OMI conducted as many villages in the area were only accessible by boat or dirt track.

Recognizing the need for a formal local organization to carry out its multiple projects and ensure the correct legal footing, in 1976 Fr. Charlie founded Yayasan Sosial Bina Sejahtera (YSBS, which means "the Foundation for bringing about Prosperity and Goodwill" in Indonesian). Since then, Fr. Charlie, a colorful character with a mixture of Irish charm and shrewd entrepreneurialism, has grown the foundation to a point where it now supports numerous projects that help the community and its surrounding areas. Similar to CCT

---

[22] Palugod, *Toward the Abundant Life*, 131.

[23] Ika Krismantari, "Romo Carolus: Inclusive Priest for Everyone," *The Jakarta Post*, 1 June 2012, http://www.thejakartapost.com/news/2012/06/01/romo-carolus-inclusive-priest-everyone.html (accessed 4 January 2014).

discussed in the previous section, YSBS seeks to address the fundamental needs of its beneficiaries through a multi-pronged approach, which includes programs aimed at poverty reduction, food security, gender issues, education, public health, climate change, and interfaith dialogue. On this last point, Fr. Charlie has been instrumental in bringing together the different religious groups in the Cilacap area to such an extent that in 2012 the Maarif Institute for Culture and Humanity, an organization that promotes using Islamic values to encourage interreligious dialogue and cooperation, gave him its annual award for his pluralistic approach toward humanitarianism.[24] While his schools, which teach in heavily Muslim communities,[25] offer courses in Islam and allow female students to wear the hijab, something unheard of in Catholic schools, he has drawn criticism from Catholic bishops over the years for not converting people. His response has been highly unusual for a Catholic priest, "Our love should come with no conditions or agendas ... I don't have any right to influence people [to convert] ... religion is a private matter between God and each individual. I don't have the right to interfere."[26]

Also uncharacteristic of a Catholic priest is Fr. Charlie's flair for entrepreneurialism. In the early days, he scraped together enough funding to build four small houses, renting them out and using the rental proceeds to slowly acquire a fleet of trucks. Initially, he used the trucks to construct roads and bridges for connecting rural villages up to Cilacap. Eventually, he acquired a large enough fleet to haul materials for profit. These profits were then used to subsidize some of the foundation's operations. For example, their charity and health division has been involved in many activities including surgeries for prosthetic limbs, cysts, and cleft lips, wheelchairs for the disabled, and transgender counseling. In 1980, YSBS started the

---

[24] Robertus Sutriyono, "Priest's Social Work Earns Muslim Award," *UCANEWS. com*, 28 May 2012, http://www.ucanews.com/news/priest%E2%80%99s-social-work-earns-muslim-award/50501 (accessed 5 January 2014).

[25] A 2010 Pew Research Center report puts the number or Muslims in Indonesia at 88%, though the figure for the island of Java, where Cilacap is located, is much higher (unofficially estimated at 96%). See http://www.pewforum.org/2010/11/04/muslim-population-of-indonesia/ (accessed 5 January 2014).

[26] Ika Krismantari, "Romo Carolus: Inclusive Priest for Everyone."

Minomartani project as a child sponsorship and nutrition program in partnership with Child Fund, which has since served 1,700 children. The foundation is also involved in reforesting land on the island of Nusakambangan, off the coast of Cilacap. The 12,500 hectare island, which is home to seven prisons, is being reforested under the direction of the foundation in a joint venture with the Department of Justice. The foundation manages the flora and fauna on the island through sustainable agriculture efforts. The following sections describe two additional programs in detail that form the core of the foundation's work.

Education

There are two types of senior high schools in Indonesia: Sekolah Menengah Atas that is generally thought of as a preparatory high school for university education, and Sekolah Menengah Kejuruan, a vocational high school that prepares students for work upon graduation. YSBS has set up five of each type of high school in the Cilacap region, along with six kindergartens, two primary schools, and seven junior high schools. YSBS schools are public and follow the national curriculum, educating approximately 5,500 students at any given time. The foundation has some ability to modify its system, and Fr. Charlie is committed to providing students with a balanced education—focusing on not only academics but also teaching students thoughtfulness, tolerance, and compassion.

At the junior and senior high school levels, YSBS cultivates interfaith dialogue and celebrates all major religious holidays. While the schools are secular, they offer Muslim, Catholic, and Protestant classes, representing the three major faiths in the area. Teaching respect, community service, and how to live in a multicultural and multi-religious environment is important to YSBS. At the lower levels, YSBS aims to serve special needs children, while teaching other children how to accept differences. Roughly sixty special needs children attend YSBS schools including autistic children (accompanied by a relative) at the kindergarten level.

YSBS's five vocational schools offer different specialized training curricula including programs in light automotive, farming, fisheries, accounting, and sewing. Sidareja is the oldest and largest school; it began in 1981 and teaches approximately 1,200 students per year.

The Majenang and Kawunganten schools began operations in 1983, while the Sokaraja and Jeruklegi schools came later in 2010. In total, all five schools educate approximately 2,100 students per year. The vocational schools have three-year programs, with a mix of theoretical and practical training. Each school has connections with industry and offers job placement services. For example, the Sidareja school places roughly seventy five percent of students into jobs, while fifteen percent of students look for work themselves, and ten percent go on to higher studies.

In the Cilacap region, a significant number of students drop out before reaching senior high school primarily because their families can no longer afford tuition.[27] In fact, less than half of primary school students matriculate to senior high school. While the Indonesian national government offers some financial assistance to poor families, it is not enough. YSBS has been able to channel both grants and zero percent social investment loans to some of its students in the form of tuition assistance and interest-free loans. Additionally, YSBS has provided financial assistance to hundreds of students through a unique goat/sheep scholarship program, which also teaches students responsibility, at one of its vocational high schools. Through this program, a goat or sheep owned by the school is given to a student to look after, the animal is impregnated and the student cares for it. When the animal gives birth, the baby is sold and the income goes to the student to pay for his or her education.

Akademi Maritim Nusantara

No discussion of the work of Fr. Charlie and YSBS's educational programs should omit mention of the maritime institute of Akademi Maritim Nusantara (AMN) located in central Cilacap. In 1991, the Indonesian government asked Fr. Charlie to take over the then-struggling institution. With a grant of five million Euros, he erected a nine-story building designed in the shape of a ship, with the upper story a complete replica of a ship's bridge overlooking the water a few miles away. Here, the cadets train in a real world "simulator" environment that prepares them for life at sea. Given Indonesia's geographical position as an archipelago of islands, and its long history of providing seafaring professions to its population, the school taps

---

[27] Primary and Secondary schools are not free in Indonesia.

into this long history and serves as a primary feeder for deck officer positions for international maritime organizations. YSBS's offices occupy the same building as well, in addition to the microfinance banks described in the next section.

Serving 600 students a year from all over Indonesia, AMN teaches three main tracks: ship engineering, nautical science, and maritime economics. After three years, students receive a Diploma III, the equivalent of a Bachelors degree. AMN is audited by the International Maritime Organization, and many of its thirty seven teachers are retired maritime officers who have a passion for passing on their knowledge and work at AMN for fairly low salaries. Most of the students receive some form of financial aid, with many taking out interest-free student loans they pay back through post-graduate employment, which is close to 100%. The school, like other YSBS schools, encourages interfaith dialogue, and has three religious teachers for Islam, Catholic, and Protestant faiths.

Microfinance

In 2009, YSBS established a women's self-help microfinance program Kelompok Swadaya Wanita or KSW ("Women's Self Help Groups") with the objective of increasing family incomes and empowering women. Catholic Relief Services helped the Foundation set up KSW, and provided training to account officers. It serves approximately two thousand women at a time, providing them with access to microfinance through a member-owned cooperative Koperasi su Kasih Ibu ("Mother's Love Cooperative"). Within the cooperative, members are formed into groups with a minimum of 15 members. Members conduct internal savings and loans activities overseen by KSW, with each group self-selecting its members and also electing its leader, treasurer, and secretary. Financial literacy and women's empowerment are key goals of KSW and this is achieved through training and mentoring to support a woman's business and financial role in her family, and by also providing opportunities for leadership positions within her group.

YSBS also has equity stakes in two Indonesian people's banks. The people's bank, Bank Perkreditan Rakyat (BPR) Ukabima Sejahtera, located on the same site as the foundation was originally founded in 2005 by Catholic Relief Services and later sold to YSBS. YSBS also has a stake in the BPR BMMS (Bina Masyarakat Mandiri Sejahtera)—also operated by Ukabima. The profits from both banks are used to subsidize the foundation's other programs.

Asasah (Lahore, Pakistan)

Given that ninety eight percent of Pakistan's population is Muslim, the main challenge is how microfinance institutions can design products that respect Sharia law. In countries such as Iraq, Sharia compliance is compulsory for all financial products. However, this often translates into inferior upfront fee models such as *Joala* (mentioned in Chapter 5) that shift nearly all the risk onto the client. Interestingly, of the dozens of microfinance institutions operating in Pakistan, only a few offer Sharia compliant products and even among those institutions those products represent merely a fraction of their portfolios. One microfinance institution has a hundred percent of its portfolio in Sharia complains products. Based out of Lahore, Pakistan, Asasah (whose name means "assets" in the local language of Urdu) is a microfinance institution founded in 2003 to "improve the living standards of very poor people, safeguard the interests of stakeholders, improve community well-being, keep employees motivated through capacity building."[28]

The three Islamic products Asasah offers are *murabaha, musharaka,* and one named *qarz-e-hasna* (an Urdu rendering of *qard hassan*) product. The *musharaka* product is a joint venture between Asasah and its client, while the *qarz-e-hasna* product is targeted to the extreme poor because it is a hundred percent free loan to the client. The *musharaka* product is divided into two main types: temporary and diminishing *musharaka*—both targeted to women. The temporary *musharaku* product is designed primarily to support home-based handloom ventures over a short time period (normally eight months). This product is primarily targeted to indentured servants living in the Swat district—a very challenging area to serve given the heavy presence of the Taliban. The diminishing *musharaka* product calls for a slow equity transfer to the client over time as the business venture becomes sustainable. This product is being piloted to support grocery

---

[28] Mixmarket.org, "MFI Report: Asasah," http://www.mixmarket.org/mfi/asasah (accessed 5 January 2014).

store ventures, and the hope is that Asasah can expand it to other types of businesses over time. For both products, the client receives technical advisory services through Asasah, including trainings in business management, bookkeeping, and adult literacy. Profits are split such that eighty percent of net profits go to the client. Any losses are borne by both Asasah and clients based on the outstanding proportion of share capital. Asasah stands out not only in Pakistan, but among worldwide microfinance institutions for offering difficult-to-implement Sharia compliant products that both place a high level of risk on Asasah and increase its operating costs.

In addition to credit products, Asasah offers a wide range of services to meet the needs of its clients. It provides business enterprise services that focus on helping clients to improve and market their products. These include helping clients to form market linkages by facilitating their attendance at exhibitions where they can present their products. Asasah is to be particularly commended for its promotion of savings to clients. Through a partnership with Tameer Bank, it has introduced three savings products, which clients can access through ATMs. The savings accounts are particularly valuable because small deposits are allowed, enabling even the poorest clients to create a financial cushion for themselves and their families.

The organization as a whole is focused on the empowerment of women and all clients are women, a marginalized group in Pakistan. Asasah also offers a number of services that specifically address the needs of women and their families. Examples include educational scholarships for the children of clients and legal advocacy services for the victims of domestic violence. In collaboration with the First Microfinance Insurance Agency (FMiA), Asasah offers a health insurance product specifically tailored towards the needs of women.

Agro Capital Management (Simferopol, Ukraine)

Agro Capital Management (ACM) was established in 2009 by Sarona Asset Management, a division of the Mennonite Economic Development Associates (MEDA). The inspiration for ACM springs from the Mennonite religious community and their historical connection to Southern Ukraine. The history of the Mennonites dates back to the Anabaptist movement (those who believed in baptizing adult believers) during the sixteenth century, at the height of the

Protestant Reformation in Europe. The Mennonites took their name from Menno Simons, a Dutch priest who converted to the Anabaptist faith and led the radical sect that swept Western and Central Europe, reaching as far as the Ukraine and Russia. Following a war with the Ottoman Empire, the Russian Emperor Catherine the Great (1729–1796) invited the Mennonites living in Prussia to farm recently acquired lands she had gained north of the Black Sea, in the Crimean peninsula and what is now Southern Ukraine. Their crops flourished in the milder climate and rich soil, and soon the Mennonites became among the wealthiest landowners in the area.

By the end of the sixteenth century, the Amish sect, a more conservative wing of Anabaptists, had broken away from the Mennonites. Both the Mennonites and their Amish cousins fled to North America and other parts of the world as a result of immediate and ongoing religious persecution throughout Europe. This persecution continued as late as the twentieth century. During the Russian Civil War (1917–1921), the Bolsheviks pushed many of the wealthy Mennonites out of the Ukraine. Another wave of persecution came after the Nazis were driven out of the Ukraine and Crimea, land that the German Army had gained during their initial Russian offensive during World War II. Many Mennonites of German ethnicity fled with the German Army as the Russian Red Army advanced into the Ukraine and the Crimean, with those Mennonites being accepted back into Germany as *Volksdeutsche*.[29] Most of the remaining Mennonites in Russia fell under heavy suspicion and were deemed Nazi collaborators who were then shipped off to Siberia and Kazakhstan, while others escaped and landed in Paraguay as refugees.

Unlike the Amish settlers who practice separatism and shun modern society and its electrical conveniences, most Mennonite settlers have slowly assimilated into their host societies, with many achieving prominence in business.[30] As of 2012, there were over 1.7 million Mennonites living in eighty two countries around the world, with the largest populations living in the United States, Canada, India,

---

[29] A term used by the Nazi government for those ethnic Germans residing outside of Germany.

[30] John D. Roth, "Mennonite Church: History," http://history.mennonite.net/ (accessed 5 January 2014).

Ethiopia, and the Democratic Republic of the Congo.[31] With a stead-fast commitment to pacifism and helping others, many wealthy Mennonites have channeled their economic resources into funding foreign aid and other charitable programs, particularly in areas where other Mennonites have settled. Their first major effort at international engagement outside of charity came from a group of Mennonite businessmen in North America who formed the MEDA to provide access to investment capital to the Russian Mennonite refugees in Paraguay in order to start new businesses—starting with a dairy farm named "Sarona" in 1954.[32]

After fifteen years of providing investment capital (mainly through joint ventures) and advisory services in Paraguay, MEDA began to branch out not only into other parts of Latin America, but also in Africa and Asia. Over time, the work of MEDA has shifted away from targeting other Mennonites, but to helping people of all religious persuasions. Turning their sites on Eastern Europe, in 2008 MEDA began searching for ways to revitalize the Southern Ukraine, particularly the Crimean peninsula. The area, with its historical Mennonite connection, once served as the bread-basket of the region before the Soviets reduced it to undifferentiated collectivized farms. In 2009, MEDA established ACM to provide agricultural financing opportunities to both small- and medium-scale farmers in Ukraine. Based in Simferopol, the administrative capital of the Crimea, ACM sells agricultural packages to farmers in the Crimea and Zaporizhia regions through a collateralized deferred-payment mechanism that links repayments with future cash flows.[33]

ACM works closely with the Ukraine Horticulture Development Project (UHDP), which assists small holder farmers in developing their agricultural businesses and participating profitably in higher value horticultural markets. The project is implemented in the

---

[31] *Mennonite World Review,* "Two-thirds World: What We Learn from MWC's Membership Census," 4 March 2013, http://www.mennoworld.org/2013/3/4/ two-thirds-world/ (accessed 5 January 2014).
[32] Mennonite Economic Development Associations (MEDA), "MEDA Timeline 1953–2000," http://www.meda.org/timeline-history (accessed 5 January 2014).
[33] After the Russian annexation of the Crimea in 2014, ACM had to suspend its operations on the peninsula and refocus its efforts to other parts of the Ukraine. Agro Capital Management, "About Agro Capital Management," http://agro capital.com.ua/index.php/en/about-acm/who-we-are (accessed 5 January 2014).

Crimea and Zaporizhia regions in cooperation with the Ukrainian government and the Canadian International Development Agency (CIDA). UHDP provides its participants with technological and informational support for horticultural business, consulting on post-harvest processing, storing and selling. The project also actively focuses on value chain development and the establishment of lead-farmer networks as a bridge between small farmers and agribusinesses. Lead farmers are provided additional education and training so that they can mentor small farmers to enhance production methods.

ACM also works in close collaboration with two major farming associations that provide seminars, sales leads, and onsite technical assistance to ACM clients. ACM's products include table grape and strawberry packages, small agricultural machinery, and larger scale equipment such as greenhouses and cold storage facilities. Currently, ACM's clients that qualify as Small Holder Farmers (farming less than five hectares of land) also benefit from a twenty five percent discount on their purchases, funded by CIDA's Canadian Investment Fund. Clients have access to training seminars and even a hotline phone number they can call to pose questions to agriculture experts. ACM's innovation in agriculture extends beyond just the products themselves. For example, it employs SMS technology to provide regular updates to its clients via their mobile phones for such things as repayment reminders for ensuring on-time repayments.

Many of ACM's clients come from the ethnic Tatar Muslim minority populations in the Crimea[34] who appreciate the Sharia compliant nature of this product (its lease-to-own contracts closely resemble *ijara* leasing products discussed in Chapter 5). However, the organization does not tout the Sharia aspect of its product structure. One reason for this is because it would require an expensive *fatwa*[35] for doing so (potentially costing thousands of dollars). But the other reason is that the product was not designed to be considered Sharia compliant per se, but rather to conform to ethical standards for financing set forth by the organization—which coincidentally conforms to Sharia

---

[34] Similar to the persecution of Mennonites following World War II, Tatars, who had a long history in the Crimea, were banished by Stalin to eastern Soviet Republics—primarily Tajikistan and Kyrgyzstan. Following the collapse of the Soviet Union, many ethnic Tatars returned to the Crimea to reestablish their communities.

[35] Religious legal opinion rendered by an Islamic jurist.

principles. In terms of both product design and the relationship of the parent organization, ACM serves as an excellent illustration of moving beyond religious inspiration and capturing universal principles such as justice in human relations. Here we see that the Mennonites have channeled the resources of their own community to help others in ways that respect their inherent worth and dignity, without the need for an enduring religious connection to the beneficiaries of their help.

What about Buddhism?

The Kachin State of northern Myanmar has seen decades of civil strife since Myanmar won independence from Britain in 1948. The Kachin people are an ethnic minority population (primarily Christian) within a country dominated by the Bamar ethnic group (primarily Buddhist). Ongoing ethnic fighting between the Kachin Independence Army and soldiers from the Myanmar government has reduced the state to poverty and despair. In 1998, the Metta Development Foundation was established as a nongovernmental organization in order to provide assistance to affected areas through building community capacity, coordinating sustainable development projects, and promoting community-controlled social and economic associations.[36]

Metta has also sponsored hundreds of village savings and loan associations throughout the Kachin State communities that it serves. It is unique in that administrative branches are located at Buddhist monasteries where monks act as facilitators to support the associations as they learn to manage their own affairs. With roughly 500–1,000 members in each association, weekly meetings at the monastery serve as training and education venues as well as centers for financial inclusion. Serving more than 140,000 people in total, many living in rural areas not served by any other financial institutions, Metta hopes to increase its reach throughout the rest of Myanmar—a country desperately trying to make its way back into the world community.

---

[36] Metta Development Foundation, "Metta Programs," http://www.metta-myanmar.org/programmes.htm (accessed 30 January 2014).

7
Can God and Mammon Work Together?

> "The quest for an enduring center is at the heart of religion. And the religious urge, I believe, is at the heart of every person—we are all religious."[1]
>
> Rev. Dr Fredric J. Muir

For many the love of money is indeed the root of all evil. Under this worldview, greed is the expression of a lack of a healthy limit on the amount of wealth a person needs to pursue happiness. Preachers can damn avarice and slam their fists on the pulpit all they want, while *The New York Times* publishes persuasive articles about the greed of the big banks, but these actions by themselves will likely do little to move the needle on an evolutionary legacy that has developed into a fundamental aspect of human nature. Observant parents first notice this when their grateful and giving babies suddenly shift into toddlers whose *perceived* lack of resources triggers overcompensation: prompted by scenes such as a toy in the corner of the room that becomes extremely valuable *only* after another child takes an interest in it. Some children are more receptive to lessons in sharing, gratitude, and how to set limits on their own desires. But for a multitude of reasons, this sometimes Sisyphean task fails to stem budding greed—particularly when a child's environment sends precisely the opposite messages that reinforce greed as a necessary value for survival. One way to erode and hopefully break the hold this

---

[1] Fredric J. Muir, *Heretic's Faith: Vocabulary for Religious Liberals* (Annapolis, MD: Unitarian Universalist Church of Annapolis, 2001), 99.

cycle of greed has on children is to teach them to give back to their communities—to be generous with their neighbors, both near and far. This can best be done by habitually modeling this sort of behavior in our daily lives. Actions overcome the limitations of words.

Similar to the multifaceted nature of human beings, this love of money also has at least one other side to it. For many it holds the promise of a better life for their families. The subtle, but important difference here is a desire for *access* to money rather than merely acquiring it to buy more things or to fill a gaping hole in one's psyche. This is particularly true among the poorest people around the world stuck navigating byzantine financial systems that more resemble perilous labyrinths than dispensers of good fortune to the clever and industrious. Opportunity is not universal—but it should be. Everyone should have the opportunity to put their talents and energies towards fully flourishing as a human being. They may not achieve it, but the burden on governments and societies ought to be to create viable avenues for everyone to follow their dreams without having to pay off corrupt officials or to lose those dreams over geography, religion, gender, class, or skin color. This requires appreciating the power money has for changing someone else's life in a positive manner and ensuring that their road to it is paved with justice.

The role of faith

Faith's primary responsibility is to inspire people to access their own *spiritual capital* for the benefit of everyone—not just the person accessing it. This spiritual capital is not limited to people belonging to faith communities. Everyone has it, and we see its expressions in the public sphere through catchphrases such as budgets being regarded as "moral documents." The link between economics and the soul sheds its obscurity when one considers that the word "economics" is literally defined as the management of a household[2]— and that a household is ultimately made up of people compelled to consider who is included in their household and where along their own road to happiness the happiness of those around them comes in. Without this, society might regress back to a Medieval or Hobbesian view of the world where independent fiefdoms compete

---

[2] Ancient Greek: οἰκονομία. From "oikos" (house) and "nomos" (law or custom).

in a struggle for survival—a condition our world persistently skirts with dangerous proximity. Nonetheless, faith communities retain a valuable vantage point for helping to connect people and financial resources to those who need it most because of their own access to and focus on spiritual capital positioned within the souls of their membership.

To further answer the question of how faith intersects with economics, particularly economics for the poor, we first need to examine the quote at the beginning of this chapter. Its words may ring true for some readers but not others. This could be attributed to differing belief systems, but it may also hinge on simple semantics. It is true that the words "faith," "religion," and "theology" often evoke intense images in the mind and those images can make it challenging to find mutually agreed upon definitions. This book has specifically avoided that route for the sake of discussion, and thus leaving it to the reader to determine his or her own definitions. However, much of the subject of religion and the religious urge in the above quote relates back more to the quest for an enduring center. Whether that enduring center is named "God," "Higher Power," or "Prime Mover" in a theistic sense or the "Universe," "Tao," or even "The Force" as one approaches a more pantheistic philosophy,[3] the desire people have to connect to something spiritual is omnipresent and persistent throughout the world among both religious and non-religious people. The ubiquitous and increasing identification with the phrase "spiritual but not religious" emphasizes the notion that most people are not yet ready to give up the idea of having a connection with something that provides meaning in their lives, regardless of how certain they are of the source of that meaning.

While religious groups have tried to attract people to a specific source and/or path of personal meaning, various philosophers and schools of psychology have also attempted to pin these down. Chapter 1 introduced the reader to Aristotle's philosophical notion of eudaimonia as our ultimate aim—striving towards a state of fully flourishing as a human being. Freud believed that aim was a *will to*

---

[3] The belief that there is no separate God or gods outside of the physical universe, but that the physical universe is its equivalent (i.e. everything is divine). Not to be confused with atheism, which contends that there is no God, gods, or a divine aspect to life.

pleasure, with sexual motivations as the primary driver of our behavior. In his book *Civilization and its Discontents*, he blasts religion, particularly Christianity, as misinterpreting the "oceanic feeling" of the divine connection—where one feels at one with the universe—which he regards as merely a longing for paternal protection in childhood that continues into adult life as a sustained "fear of the superior power of Fate."[4] He rejects loving one's neighbor as oneself because he believes that people must first be deserving of someone else's love and it is not to be given without condition.[5] Alfred Adler's rival Viennese school of psychology countered Freud's will to *pleasure* with a will to *power* as the ultimate aim of human beings. Adler's view was not the same as Nietzsche's own will to power characterized as a desire to dominate others, but rather a will to create and achieve personal perfection—placing it closer to Aristotle's eudaimonia.

Adler's former pupil, Viktor Frankl, a survivor of the Nazi concentration camps and author of *Man's Search for Meaning*—both a personal account of his experiences in the camps and an introduction to his school of psychology—outlines his third view of a *will to meaning* as the primary motivational force in human beings.[6] He saw this striving towards meaning in one's life played out in the camps as prisoners struggled with a determination to stay alive amid some of the harshest conditions that human beings have ever had to endure. Frankl noticed that those who strove to fulfill a meaning in their lives and had found a "why" to live, however small, fared much better than others who felt they had nothing left in this world.[7] This was most true of people with a deeply held faith.[8] Frankl himself found meaning in recording on small scraps of paper his thoughts and ideas for rewriting the book manuscript he was forced to give up upon arriving at Auschwitz—his will to live driven by a desire to see his creation come to fruition. Those with nothing to look forward to after their potential future release from the camp were often doomed to complete despair. Since items like cigarettes were so

[4] Sigmund Freud, *Civilization and its Discontents,* trans. James Strachey (New York: W.W. Norton, 1989), 20.
[5] Freud, *Civilization and its Discontents,* 66.
[6] Victor Frankl, *Man's Search for Meaning* (New York: Simon & Schuster, 1984), 104.
[7] Frankl, *Man's Search for Meaning,* 109.
[8] Frankl, *Man's Search for Meaning,* 47.

valuable because they could be traded for a precious bowl of soup, a prisoner seen smoking was a sure sign that they had given up on life and would soon die.[9]

Of course, this search for meaning is not restricted to those caught in a desperate situation and it applies to all human beings. Furthermore, Frankl cautions people not to strive for a homeostatic condition, since achieving one would only lead to boredom and possible depression.[10] On the surface, this contradicts so many teachings that call on us to attain a peaceful state of mind without any internal conflict. However, it better reflects the condition of human beings, taking account of our psychological complexities and a universal desire to strive towards goals. For Frankl, each of us needs to channel this striving to seek meaning in our daily lives through one or more of the following: creativity, deeds, experiencing something, encountering someone, or by the attitude we take toward unavoidable suffering.[11] The last one seems particularly challenging, but certainly powerful given that much of life contains periods of unavoidable suffering that provide opportunities to turn those sufferings into personal triumphs. Frankl's *will to meaning* indeed coalesces with both Aristotle's eudaimonia and virtue ethics discussed in Chapter 1 since meaning is derived from making the best choices that lead towards that which one is striving towards: always moving from potential states to actual states through thoughtful action.

How to learn what would make meaning in our lives is among the ultimate questions that cannot be answered by a single statement or even a long treatise on what has worked for a single individual. For many people, it is an unfolding process that comes about through meditation, prayer, or other forms of spiritual activity that at some point may involve quieting the mind and listening to an inner voice that guides us once we are able to tune out our seemingly incessant mind-chatter. For some, the spark of clarity arrives in an instant and without advanced warning. At times this comes about through unexpected mediums such as music, art, or the words of a great writer whose metaphor penetrates the depths of one's soul. Homer likened this to the gods *breathing* inspiration into the soul of a hesitant hero

---

[9] Frankl, *Man's Search for Meaning*, 21.
[10] Frankl, *Man's Search for Meaning*, 110.
[11] Frankl, *Man's Search for Meaning*, 115.

to give him courage and recognition of the clear path forward. For example, while fighting for their lives against the Cyclops, Odysseus remarks on the crew's sudden rise in strength and resolve, "Some great divinity breathed courage into us (Book 9, Line 381)."[12]

Whether one believes that an inspiration that reveals meaning comes from inside or outside (or both), a central question Chapter 1 of this book has wrestled with is whether or not that meaning includes helping others—particularly the poor and less fortunate. After exploring the spiritual and philosophical arguments for helping others, Chapter 2 introduced readers to historical and contemporary economic development methods that arguably help the poor find meaning in their lives by giving them the ability to chart their own future through increased access to finance. Some readers might be asking how they can personally connect a motivation to create meaning in their own lives by helping others through supporting microfinance efforts. The common thread of the organizations discussed in the previous chapter is that they are all partners of Kiva Microfunds, an organization that gives everyday people the opportunity to support poverty alleviation efforts all over the world in a way that captures the spirit of Maimonides' highest level of giving mentioned early on in this book (i.e. to give someone in need a loan at zero percent interest).

As a promoter and facilitator of microfinance, the mission of Kiva is to connect people through lending to alleviate poverty. A nonprofit organization founded in 2005 and based in the United Sates, Kiva works with a burgeoning network of hundreds of partners in over seventy countries around the world, allowing them to raise funds for microfinance loans on its Internet platform. Kiva employs a crowd-sourcing, peer-to-peer model where lenders can visit the website and contribute as little as twenty five dollars towards an interest-free loan for a specific client posted on the platform whose picture and story they find compelling. By 2013, Kiva lenders had funded half a billion dollars in loans, helping to serve over a million of the world's poor. Lenders do not earn a financial return, but simply receive the principle back if and when the client repays. Kiva's overall repayment rate hovers near ninety nine percent, proving that microfinance clients remain a low credit risk.

---

[12] Homer and Richmond Alexander Lattimore, *The Odyssey of Homer* (New York: HarperPerennial, 1991), 147.

While Kiva does not charge an interest rate to the clients posted on the site, most of its partners indeed charge on the loans that they make. The high transactional costs associated with servicing loans, particularly to poor borrowers in rural areas, are exactly why those same borrowers have not been served by the traditional banking system. This point has been discussed throughout this book. So, in terms of assessing responsible pricing, the main question is whether or not those microfinance institutions are striking a healthy balance between financial sustainability and treatment of clients. So, Kiva takes a strong interest in making certain it maintains the right relationships with partners that are aligned with its own values of fair and responsible pricing. Kiva has also made great strides in supporting partners that offer a range of financial and non-financial services, as well as loan products that increase the risk-sharing level between partners and their clients—something touched upon in the previous chapter. To learn more about Kiva and to make a loan, please visit its website here: www.kiva.org.

As Kiva's regional director managing the partner relationships in Europe and Asia for the past several years, I have been fortunate to see first-hand both the power of microfinance to transform people's lives and the role faith has played in the sector. The intersection of faith and international economic development is fascinating for its power to channel spiritual motivation in a way that allows God and mammon to work together for the sake of the poorest of the poor. It is also an area that requires persistent inquiry into the various expressions of those spiritual motivations. As the middle chapters of this book have shown, religious influences can be both overt and subtle—even within a secular context. Max Weber's suggestion, mentioned in Chapter 3 and worth repeating, that many people continue to remain stuck in an "iron cage" of capitalism while the spirit of religious asceticism has long escaped the cage,[13] resonates with modern America and presents a distinct challenge in international economic development and anywhere philanthropic capital chases after solutions to poverty. While microfinance can have lasting positive effects on the lives of the poor, we should be watchful of just how much of the American dream we export to places that need methods and

---

[13] Max Weber, *The Protestant Ethic and the Spirit of Capitalism* (Mineola, NY: Dover Publications, 2003), 181.

models that take into account their own cultural needs. Ultimately, microfinance can best serve the poor by inspiring people to give their time and resources to promoting ways that inspire clients to build up solid foundations that ensure that not only those clients, but also their children escape poverty and fully flourish as human beings with dignity and respect.

Father Charlie Burrows, O.M.I. presiding over mass in Cilacap, Indonesia
Photo Credit: © 2013 Teresa Yung

Father Charlie Burrows at the SMK Yos Soedarso Sidareja vocational school
outside Cilacap, Indonesia
Photo Credit: © 2012 Michael Looft

Akademi Maritim Nusantana in Cilacap, Indonesia
Photo Credit: © 2013 Teresa Yung

The bridge atop Akademi Maritim Nusantana in Cilacap, Indonesia
Photo Credit: © 2013 Teresa Yung

Computer lab at the SMK Yos Soedarso Kawunganten vocational School outside Cilacap, Indonesia
Photo Credit: © 2013 Michael Mazur

Student at the SMK Yos Soedarso Kawunganten vocational school outside Cilacap, Indonesia
Photo Credit: © 2012 Yayasan Sosial Bina Sejahtera

Purified water refilling station in Manila, Philippines (Center for Community Transformation)
Photo Credit: © 2013 Michael Mazur

Shopkeeper and client of Center for Community Transformation in Manila, Philippines
Photo Credit: © 2013 Teresa Yung

Leroy Lamiseria, former street dweller, who now works as a construction worker with the help of the Center for Community Transformation's Kaibigan (Friend) Ministry.
Photo Credit: © 2012 Center for Community Transformation

Former street children and now students at Center for Community Transformation's Visions of Hope Christian School in Laguna, Philippines
Photo Credit: © 2012 Arthur M. Trinidad

Agricultural training in the Crimea
Photo Credit: © 2014 Kiva Microfunds

Small-hold farmer and client of Agro Capital Management in the Crimea
Photo Credit: © 2014 Kiva Microfunds

Small-hold farmer and client of Agro Capital Management in the Crimea
Photo Credit: © 2014 Kiva Microfunds

Small-hold farmer market in Simferopol, Crimea
Photo Credit: © 2014 Kiva Microfunds

Harvest festival in the Crimea
Photo Credit: © 2014 Kiva Microfunds

Fruits and vegetables produced by Agro Capital Management clients in the Crimea
Photo Credit: © 2014 Kiva Microfunds

Asasah *Qarz-e-Hasna* (interest-free loan) women's group in Swat district of Pakistan
Photo Credit: © 2013 Asasah

Asasah's *Musharaka* profit sharing program with hand weavers in Lahore, Pakistan
Photo Credit: © 2013 Asasah

Food Security Program of Asasah in Punjab province of Pakistan
Photo Credit: © 2013 Asasah

Thread weaver and client of Asasah in Swat district of Pakistan
Photo Credit: © 2013 Asasah

Asasah *Musharaka* financed client in Swat district of Pakistan
Photo Credit: © 2013 Asasah

Bibliography

Samuel O. Abogunrin (Gen. Editor), J.O. Akao, D.O. Akintunde, D. Kunle, G.N. Toryough and P.A. Oguntoye (2007) (Eds) *Biblical Studies and Corruption in Africa*. Biblical Studies Series No.6. Ibadan: NABIS, p. 654.

ACCION. "About Us." http://www.accion.org/about-us (accessed 31 December 2013).

ACCION. "Our History." http://www.accion.org/about-us/history/1970s (accessed 31 December 2013).

Agro Capital Management. "About Agro Capital Management." http://agrocapital.com.ua/index.php/en/about-acm/who-we-are (accessed 5 January 2014).

Alexander, Anne. *The Antigonish Movement: Moses Coady and Adult Education Today*. Toronto: Thompson Educational Publishing, Inc., 1997.

All Great Quotes. "Lao Tzu." http://www.allgreatquotes.com/lao_tzu_quotes.shtml (accessed 31 December 2013).

Anscombe, Elizabeth. "Modern Moral Philosophy." in *Philosophy*, vol. 33, no. 124 (January 1958).

Aristotle and M. Ostwald. *Nicomachean Ethics*. Englewood Cliffs, NJ: Prentice Hall, 1992.

Armendáriz de Aghion, Beatriz and J. Morduch. *The Economics of Microfinance*. Cambridge, MA: MIT Press, 2005.

Associated Press, "SKS Under Spotlight in Suicides," *The Wall Street Journal*, 24 February 2012, http://online.wsj.com/article/SB10001424052970203918304577242602296683134.html (accessed 3 January 2014).

Bajaj, Vikas. "Microlender, First in India to Go Public, Trades Higher." *The New York Times*, 16 August 2010. http://www.nytimes.com/2010/08/17/business/global/17micro.html?_r=0 (accessed 3 January 2014).

Bakhtiar, Abbas. "Ahmadinejad's Achilles Heel: The Iranian Economy." *Payvand's Iran News*, 25 January 2007. http://www.payvand.com/news/07/jan/1295.html#_edn7 (accessed 4 January 2014).

Bakker, Jim and K. Abraham. *I was wrong*. Nashville: T. Nelson, 1996.

Ballard, Melvin Russell. "Becoming Self-Reliant—Spiritually and Physically." (address given at Brigham Young University during the opening of the Marriott School's Center for Economic Self-Reliance, Provo, Utah, 11 March 2004).

Banerjee, Abhijit V. and E. Duflo. *Poor Economics*. New York: Public Affairs, 2001.

Bornstein, Erica. *The Spirit of Development: Protestant NGOs, Morality, and Economics in Zimbabwe*. Stanford, CA: Stanford University Press, 2005.

Buckley, Susan L. *Teachings on Usury in Judaism, Christianity and Islam*. Lewiston, NY: The Edwin Mellen Press, 2000.

Bushman, Richard L. *Joseph Smith: Rough Stone Rolling*. New York: Vintage Books, 2005.

BYU Marriott School. "About Melvin J. Ballard." http://marriottschool.byu.edu/selfreliance/about/melvin (accessed 3 January 2014).

Cahill, Lisa Sowle. *Theological Bioethics: Participation, Justice, and Change*. Washington, DC: Georgetown University Press, 2005.

Caplan, Jeremy. "Microfinance Still Hums, Despite Global Financial Crisis." *Time*, 3 December 2008. http://www.time.com/time/business/article/0,8599,1863443,00.html (accessed 2 January 2013).

Catholic Relief Services, "About Catholic Relief Services," http://www.catholicrelief.org/about/ (accessed 2 January 2014).

The Catholic Worker Movement. "The Aims and Means of the Catholic Worker." http://www.catholicworker.org/aimsandmeanstext.cfm?Number=5 (accessed 31 December 2013).

The Catholic Worker Movement. "A Collection of Peter Maurin's Essays." http://www.catholicworker.org/roundtable/easyessays.cfm (accessed 4 January 2014).

The Catholic Worker Movement, "This Money is not ours" by Dorothy Day, http://www.catholicworker.org/DorothyDay/daytext.cfm?TextID=768, 6 September 1960, (accessed 31 December 2013).

Center for Community Transformation. "Community Mobilization and Empowerment." http://cct.org.ph/community-mobilization-and-empowerment/ (accessed 4 January 2014).

Center for Community Transformation. "Education." http://cct.org.ph/education/ (accessed 4 January 2014).

Center for Community Transformation. "Health." http://cct.org.ph/health/ (accessed 4 January 2014).

Center for Community Transformation. "Kaibigan Ministry." http://cct.org.ph/kaibigan-ministry/ (accessed 4 January 2014).

Center for Community Transformation. "Mission." http://cct.org.ph/about/mission/ (accessed 4 January 2014).

Center for Community Transformation. "Microfinance." http://cct.org.ph/microfinance// (accessed 4 January 2014).

Center for Community Transformation. "Vision." http://cct.org.ph/about/vision/ (accessed 4 January 2014).

Chabad.org. "Maimonides' Eight Levels of Charity." http://www.chabad.org/library/article_cdo/aid/45907/jewish/Eight-Levels-of-Charity.htm (accessed 31 December 2013).

Chernow, Ron. *Titan: The Life of John D. Rockefeller, Sr.* New York: Vintage Books, 1998.

The Church of Jesus Christ of Latter-day Saints. *The Doctrine and Covenants of the Church of Jesus Christ of Latter-Day Saints. The Pearl of Great Price.* Salt Lake City, UT: Church of Jesus Christ of Latter-Day Saints, 2013.

The Church of Jesus Christ of Latter-day Saints, "The Family: A Proclamation to the World", Available at: http://www.lds.org/library/display/0,4945,161-1-11-1,00.html (accessed 2 January 2014).

The Church of Jesus Christ of Latter-day Saints, Gospel Library: Gospel Topics, "Prophets," http://www.lds.org/ldsorg/v/index.jsp?locale=0&sourceId=c65 49c57af139010VgnVCM1000004d82620a___&vgnextoid=bbd508f54922d 010VgnVCM1000004d82620aRCRD (accessed 3 January 2014).

Cicero, Marcus Tullius and M. Grant. "On Duties II." In *On the Good Life.* Penguin Classics. Harmondsworth: Penguin, 1971.

Coady International Institute. Masters of Their Own Destiny: The Coady Story in Canada and Across the World. "The Antigonish Movement." http://coad yextension.stfx.ca/antigonish-movement/ (accessed 31 December 2013).

Coady International Institute. "Transformative Leadership Education Programs." http://coady.stfx.ca/education/ (accessed 31 December 2013).

Collier, Paul. *The Bottom Billion: Why the Poorest Countries are Failing and What Can Be Done About It.* New York: Oxford University Press, 2007.

Collins, Daryl, J. Morduch, S. Rutherford, and O. Ruthven. *Portfolios of the Poor,* Princeton, New Jersey: Princeton University Press, 2009.

Common Dreams. "Alan Shrugged: Greenspan, Ayn Rand and Their God That Failed." https://www.commondreams.org/view/2008/10/25-6 (accessed 2 January 2014).

Coville, Thierry. *The Economy of Islamic Iran: Between State and Market.* Louvain: Institut français de recherche en Iran, 1994.

Crane, Keith, R. Lal, and J. Martini. *Iran's Political, Demographic, and Economic Vulnerabilities.* Arlington, VA: Rand Corporation, 2008.

Dadwood, N. J. *The Koran.* London: Penguin Books, 1990.

Die Genossenschaften. "Cooperatives in Germany: History of cooperatives". http://www.dgrv.de/en/cooperatives/historyofcooperatives.html (accessed 31 December 2013).

Easterly, William. *White Man's Burden: Why the West's Efforts to Aid the Rest Have Done So Much Ill and So Little Good.* New York: Penguin Books, 2006.

Ellis, Stephen and Gerrie Ter Haar. *Worlds of power: Religious Thought and Political Practice in Africa.* New York: Oxford University Press, 2004.

Emerson, Ralph Waldo. *Self Reliance and Other Essays.* New York: Dover, 1993.

Evangelical Lutheran Church of America, "A Social Statement on: Sufficient, Sustainable Livelihood for All." http://download.elca.org/ELCA%20 Resource%20Repository/Economic_LifeSS.pdf (accessed 4 January 2014).

Farabi Cinema Foundation. http://www.fcf.ir/en/ (accessed 2 January 2014).

FINCA. "Our Clients." http://www.villagebanking.org/site/c.erKPI2PCIoE/ b.2630021/k.A6B6/Our_Clients.htm (accessed 2 January 2013).

Forbes.com. "Thoughts on the Business of Life" by John D Rockefeller. http:// thoughts.forbes.com/thoughts/charity-john-d-rockefeller-jr-charity-is-inju rious (accessed 31 December 2013).

Frankl, Victor. *Man's Search for Meaning.* New York: Simon & Schuster, 1984.

Freud, Sigmund. *Civilization and its Discontents.* trans. James Strachey. New York: W.W. Norton, 1989.

Galang, Regina, S. Margolin, and G. Stuart Galang and Margolin. "John F Kennedy School of Government Case Study: The Social Construction of Gender: Microfinance and *fa'afafines* in Samoa." 2005.

Geertz, Clifford. "The Rotating Credit Association: A Middle Rung in Development." http://hypergeertz.jku.at/GeertzTexts/Rotating_Credit1. htm (accessed 31 December 2013).

Gerber, Michael. *The E-Myth Revisited: Why Most Small Businesses Don't Work and What to Do About It.* New York: HarperCollins Publishers, Inc., 1995.

Gibson, Stephen W. and B. M. Gibson, *Where there are No Jobs, Volume 2.* Provo: UT: The Academy for Creating Enterprise, Date Unknown.

Graeber, David. *Debt: The First 5,000 Years.* New York: Melville House Publishing, 2011.

Grameen Bank. "Grameen Bank at a Glance." http://www.grameen-info.org/ index.php?option=com_content&task=view&id=26&Itemid=0 (accessed 31 December 2013.

Grameen Bank. "Grameen II." http://www.grameen-info.org/index. php?option=com_content&task=view&id=30&Itemid=116 (accessed 31 December 2013).

Grameen Bank. "Meet clients of Grameen Foundation partner MFIs." http:// www.grameenfoundation.org/resource_center/client_success_stories/ (accessed 2 January 2014).

Gutierrez, Gustavo. *A Theology of Liberation.* Maryknoll, New York: Orbison Books, 2012.

Harper, Malcolm. "What's Wrong with Groups." In: *What's Wrong with Microfinance?*, ed. Thomas Dichter and Malcolm Harper. Warwickshire, UK: Practical Action Publishing, 1997.

Harper, Malcolm, D. S. K. Rao, and A. K. Sahu. *Development, Divinity and Dharma: The role of Religion in Development and Microfinance Institutions.* Rugby, Warwickshire, UK: Practical Action Publishing, 2008.

Hashemi, Syed. "Beyond Good Intentions: Measuring Social Performance of Microfinance Institutions." CGAP Focus Note No. 41. Washington DC: The World Bank, May 2007.

Hebrew Free Loan Society. "History." http://www.hfls.org/about-us/history (accessed 4 January 2014).

Higgins, Andrew. "Inside Iran's Holy Money Machine." *The Wall Street Journal,* 2 June 2007. http://online.wsj.com/news/articles/SB118072271215621679 (accessed 5 January 2014).

Hoffman, Reid and B. Casnocha. *The Start-up of You: Adapt to the Future, Invest in Yourself, and Transform Your Career.* New York. Crown Business, 2012.

Hollis, Aidan. *Women and Microcredit in History, In Women and Credit: Researching the Past, Refiguring the Future.* New York: Berg, 2002.

Homer and R. A. Lattimore. *The Odyssey of Homer.* New York: Harper Perennial, 1991.

Hurst, Erik and A. Lusardi. "Do Household Savings Encourage Entrepreneurship?" In: *Overcoming Barriers to Entrepreneurship in the United States,* ed. Diana Furchgott-Roth. Lanham, MD: Lexington Books, 2008.

International Association of Jewish Free Loans, "About IAJFL," http://www. freeloan.org/about-iajfl/ (accessed 4 January 2014).

International Monetary Fund. "Islamic Republic of Iran: Staff Report for the 2004 Article IV Consultation." IMF Country Report 04/306. Washington, DC, September 2004.

Johnson, Paul. *A History of the Jews.* London: Orion Books Ltd, 1987.

Jones, Lindsay. "African Cosmologies," in *Encyclopedia of religion,* 2nd ed., Detroit: Macmillan Reference USA, 2005.

Kalu, Ogbu. *Power, Poverty, and Prayer: The Challenges of Poverty and Pluralism in African Christianity, 1960–1996.* Frankfurt: Peter Lang GmbH, 2000.

Kanovsky, Eliyahu. *Iran's Economic Morass: Mismanagement and Decline under the Islamic Republic.* Policy papers; no. 44. Washington, DC: Washington Institute for Near East Policy, 1997.

Kneiding, Christoph and R. Rosenberg. "Variations in Microcredit Interest Rates." *CGAP.org,* 1 July 2008. http://www.cgap.org/publications/variations-microcredit-interest-rates (accessed 4 January 2014).

Krismantari, Ika. "Romo Carolus: Inclusive Priest for Everyone." *The Jakarta Post,* 1 June 2012. http://www.thejakartapost.com/news/2012/06/01/romo-carolus-inclusive-priest-everyone.html (accessed 4 January 2014).

Kristof, Nicolas. "From South Sudan to Yale." *The New York Times,* 28 March 2012. http://www.nytimes.com/2012/03/29/opinion/kristof-from-south-sudan-to-yale.html?_r=0 (accessed 2 January 2014).

Leo XIII. Encyclical Letter. *Rerum Novarum* (of New Things). Vatican Website. 15 May 1891. http://www.vatican.va/holy_father/leo_xiii/encyclicals/documents/hf_l-xiii_enc_15051891_rerum-novarum_en.html (accessed 31 December 2013).

Liddell, Henry and R. Scott. *An Intermediate Greek-English Lexicon.* New York: Oxford University Press, 2001.

Lucas, James W. and W. Woodworth. *Working Toward Zion: Principles of the United Order for the Modern World.* Salt Lake City: Aspen Books, 1996.

Luther, Martin. *Luther's Works,* Volume 45, edit. Jaroslav Pelikan. St. Louis, MO: Concordia Publishing House, 1955.

Luz, Ulrich. *Studies in Matthew.* Grand Rapids, Mich.: W.B. Eerdmans Publication Company, 2005.

Malawi Human Rights Commission. "Cultural Practices and their Impact on the Enjoyment of Human Rights, Particularly the Rights of Women and Children in Malawi." Publication date unknown, (found at http://www.medcol.mw/commhealth/publications/cultural_practices_report.pdf (accessed 5 January 2014).

Maloney, Suzanne. "Politics, Patronage, and Social Justice: Parastatal Foundations and Post-Revolutionary Iran." Ph.D. Dissertation. The Fletcher School of Law and Diplomacy, 2001.

Mangum, Garth and B. Blumell, *The Mormons' War on Poverty: A History of LDS Welfare, 1830–1990,* Salt Lake City: University of Utah Press, 1993.

Manusmriti. *The Laws of Manu.* Trans. G. Buhler. Oxford, UK: Clarendon Press, 1886.

Matthews, Jessica and R. Rosenberg. *Community-Managed Loan Funds: Which Ones Work?* CGAP Focus Note, No. 36. Washington, DC: The World Bank, May 2006.

Mennonite Economic Development Associations (MEDA). "MEDA Timeline 1953–2000." http://www.meda.org/timeline-history (accessed 5 January 2014).

Mennonite World Review. "Two-thirds World: What We Learn from MWC's Membership Census." *Mennonite World Review,* 4 March 2013. http://www.mennoworld.org/2013/3/4/two-thirds-world/ (accessed 5 January 2014).

Metta Development Foundation. "Metta Programs." http://www.metta-myanmar.org/programmes.htm (accessed 30 January 2014).

Micro-Credit Ratings International. "BASIX Social Rating 2007." http://www.m-cril.com/pdf/Rating-Reports/BASIX-Social-Rating-2007-M-CRIL.pdf (accessed 2 January 2014).

The Microfinance Gateway. "The Debate About Social Performance." http://www.microfinancegateway.org/resource_centers/socialperformance/today (accessed 2 January 2014).

Mixmarket.org. "MFI Report: Asasah." http://www.mixmarket.org/mfi/asasah (accessed 5 January 2014).

Molavi, Afshin. *The Soul of Iran.* New York: Norton, 2005.

Monson, President Thomas M. "Welcome to Conference." *Liahona Magazine,* May 2013. http://www.lds.org/liahona/2013/05/welcome-to-conference (accessed 2 January 2014).

Mormon Newsroom, "Facts and Statistics." http://www.mormonnewsroom.org/facts-and-stats (accessed 2 January 2014).

Muir, Fredric J. *Heretic's Faith: Vocabulary for Religious Liberals.* Annapolis, MD: Unitarian Universalist Church of Annapolis, 2001.

Nelson, Benjamin. *The Idea of Usury: from Tribal Brotherhood to Universal Otherhood.* Chicago: University of Chicago Press, 1969.

Nibley, Hugh W. *Approaching Zion.* Salt Lake City: Deseret Book and FARMS Review, 1989. 203–51.

Nisbett, Richard E. *Geography of Thought: How Asians and Westerners Think Differently ... and Why.* New York: Free Press, 2003.

Nobelprize.org. "The Nobel Peace Prize 2006." http://nobelprize.org/nobel_prizes/peace/laureates/2006/ (accessed 31 December 2013).

Nussbaum, Martha. *Women and Human Development: The Capabilities Approach.* New York: Cambridge University Press, 2000.

Olupona, Jacob. "On Africa, A Need for Nuance." Harvard Divinity Bulletin. Autumn 2007.

Opportunity International. "Technology." http://opportunity.org/what-we-do/products-and-services/global-technology#.UXivCLXqmkI (accessed 2 January 2014).

Orlian, Rabbi Meir. "What is a Heter Iska and How Does it Work." *Jewish Press,* 13 May 2009. http://www.businesshalacha.com/articles/heter-iska-101-ipes (accessed 4 January 2014).

Palugod, Sylvia. *Toward the Abundant Life: Transforming Lives, Transforming Communities.* Manila: OMF Literature, 2008.

Parsons, Anthony. *The Pride and the Fall: Iran, 1974–1979.* London: Jonathon Cape, 1984.

Paulson, David L. and C. G. Walker. "Work Worship and Grace." Desert Books and FARMS Review, 2000. 83–127.

Pew Research Center, "Tolerance and Tension: Islam and Christianity in Sub-Saharan Africa," 15 April 2010, http://www.pewforum.org/2010/04/15/executive-summary-islam-and-christianity-in-sub-saharan-africa/ (accessed 30 May 2014).

Pew Research Center. "Christian Movements and Denominations." 19 December 2011. http://www.pewforum.org/2011/12/19/global-christianity-movements-and-denominations/ (accessed 4 January 2014).

Pew Research Center. "Overview: Pentecostalism in Latin America." 5 October 2006. http://www.pewforum.org/2006/10/05/overview-pentecostalism-in-latin-america/ (accessed 4 January 2014).

Pew Research Center. "Regional Distribution of Christians." 19 December 2011. http://www.pewforum.org/2011/12/19/global-christianity-regions/ (accessed 4 January 2014).

Pew Research Center. "Tolerance and Tension: Islam and Christianity in Sub-Saharan Africa." 15 April 2010. http://www.pewforum.org/2010/04/15/executive-summary-islam-and-christianity-in-sub-saharan-africa/ (accessed 4 January 2014).

Pius XI. Encyclical Letter. *Quadragesimo Anno* (In the 40th Year). Vatican Website. 15 May 1931. http://www.vatican.va/holy_father/pius_xi/encyclicals/documents/hf_p-xi_enc_19310515_quadragesimo-anno_en.html. sec. 110 (accessed 31 December 2013).

Raiffeisen Bank. "History of Raiffeisen Bank Group". http://www.raiffeisen.ru/en/about/bankgroup/ (accessed 31 December 2013).

Ratzinger, Joseph Cardinal. "Liberation Theology." From a private memo published in the Italian press in 1984. http://www.christendom-awake.org/pages/ratzinger/liberationtheol.htm (accessed 5 January 2014).

Roth, John D. "Mennonite Church: History," http://history.mennonite.net/ (accessed 5 January 2014).

Ruderman, David B. *The World of the Renaissance Jew: The Life and Thought of Abraham Ben Mordecai Farissol.* Cincinnati: Hebrew Union College Press, 1981.

Rutherford, Stuart. *The Poor and their Money.* New Delhi: Oxford University Press, 2000.

RWE.org. The Works of Ralph Waldo Emerson. "Chapter VII Works and Days," http://rwe.org/complete-works/vii---society-and-solitude/chapter-vii--works-and-days (accessed 2 January 2014).

Ryesky, Kenneth H. "Secular Law Enforcement of the Heter 'Iska." *JLaw.com.* http://www.jlaw.com/Articles/heter1.html (accessed 4 January 2014).

Savings-Revolution.org, "Online Savings-led Library." http://savings-revolution.org/doclib/Savings%20and%20Internal%20Lending%20Communities%20SILC%20a%20Basis%20for%20Integral%20Human%20Development.pdf (accessed 2 January 2014).

Seibel, Hans Dieter. "The Microbanking Division of Bank Rakyat Indonesia: A Flagship of Micro-finance in Asia." In: *Small Customers, Big Market: Commercial Banks in Micro-Finance.* ed. Malcolm Harper and Sukhwinder Arora. Rugby, UK: Practical Action, 2005.

Sheridan, Thomas. *The Life of the Rev. Dr. Jonathan Swift*, 2nd ed. London: Rivington, 1787.

Shipps, Jan. "The Prophet Puzzle: Suggestions Leading Toward a More Comprehensive Interpretation of Joseph Smith" *The Prophet Puzzle*. Salt Lake City: Signature Books, 1997.

Shri Mahila Sewa Sahakari Bank Ltd. "History." http://www.sewabank.com/history.html (accessed 2 January 2014).

Shri Mahila Sewa Sahakari Bank Ltd., "Latest News," http://www.sewabank.com/news-events.html (accessed 2 January 2014).

Stevenson, Howard H. "A Paradigm of Entrepreneurship." in *Strategic Management Journal*, Vol. 11. Special Issue: Corporate Entrepreneurship. Hoboken, NJ: John Wiley: Summer 1990.

Stuart, Guy: "John F Kennedy School of Government Case Study: Caste Embeddedness and Microfinance: Savings and Credit Cooperatives in Andhra Pradesh, India." September 2006. Available at: https://research.hks.harvard.edu/publications/getFile.aspx?Id=230.

Stuart, Guy: "John F Kennedy School of Government Case Study: Women's Thrift Cooperatives in Andhra Pradesh." 2002, https://research.hks.harvard.edu/publications/getFile.aspx?Id=86.

Sutriyono, Robertus. "Priest's Social Work Earns Muslim Award." *UCANEWS. com*, 28 May 2012. http://www.ucanews.com/news/priest%E2%80%99s-social-work-earns-muslim-award/50501 (accessed 5 January 2014).

Systems and Us. "How Kiva Serves the Poorest." Courtesy of Center for Community Transformation. 26 July 2012. http://systemsandus.com/2012/07/26/how-kiva-serves-the-poorest/ (accessed 5 January 2014).

Transparency International. "Corruption Perception Index 2008." http://www.transparency.org/policy_research/surveys_indices/cpi/2008 (accessed 2 January 2014).

United Labs, "Unitus, Inc. Redirects Efforts," 2 July 2010, http://unituslabs.org/updates/unitus-redirects-efforts/ (accessed 3 January 2014).

United Labs, "Unitus Teams Up with OPIC and CITI," 29 March 2010, http://unituslabs.org/updates/unitus-teams-up-with-opic-citi/ (accessed 3 January 2014).

Vancouver City Savings Credit Union."Financial Literacy and Basic Banking." https://www.vancity.com/AboutVancity/VisionAndValues/ValuesBasedBanking/FinancialLiteracyAndBasicBanking/ (accessed 31 December 2013).

Visser, Wayne A.M. and A. McIntosh. "A Short Review of the Historical Critique of Usury." in *Accounting, Business & Financial History*, Vol. 8, no. 2 (London: Routledge, July 1998).

Wallis, Jim. *God's Politics: Why the Right Gets it Wrong and the Left Doesn't Get it*. New York: HarperSanFrancisco, 2005.

Warde, Ibrahim. *Islamic Finance in the Global Economy*. Edinburgh: Edinburgh University Press, 2010.

Weaver, Sarah Jane. "Fighting Poverty: Research by BYU's Center for Economic Self-Reliance to Help Poor." *Deseret News* 76, no. 25 (2006): 8–9.

Weber, Max. *The Protestant Ethic and the Spirit of Capitalism*. Mineola, NY: Dover Publications, 2003.

Weissmann, Jordan. "Think We're the Most Entrepreneurial Country In the World? Not So Fast." *The Atlantic,* 2 October 2012. http://www.theatlantic.com/business/archive/2012/10/think-were-the-most-entrepreneurial-country-in-the-world-not-so-fast/263102/ (accessed 2 January 2014).

Wesley, John. Sermon 50: "The Use of Money." http://www.umcmission.org/Find-Resources/John-Wesley-Sermons/Sermon-50-The-Use-of-Money (accessed 2 January 2014).

Wilson, Kim. "The Moneylender's Dilemma." In *What's Wrong with Microfinance?* ed. Thomas Dichter and Malcolm Harper. Warwickshire, UK: Practical Action Publishing, 1997.

Woodworth, Warner, J. Grenny, and T. Manwaring. *United for Zion: Principles for Uniting the Saints to Eliminate Poverty,* Orem, UT: Unitus Publications, 2000.

Yunus, Muhammad. *Banker to the Poor.* New York: Public Affairs, 2003.

Index

Lightning Source UK Ltd.
Milton Keynes UK
UKOW05n0910210916

283481UK00016B/314/P